Personal Bank Statement Mortgage Loans

How to Qualify Using Personal Bank Statements Instead of Income Documents

By Joseph G. Correa

Licensed Mortgage Broker, Finibi Mortgage

Copyright & Legal Notice

Published by Live Stronger Faster

The information provided in this book is for educational and informational purposes only and does not constitute financial, legal, tax, or investment advice. Although the author is a licensed mortgage professional, the content presented is general in nature and is not intended as personalized guidance for any specific individual or financial situation.

The strategies, structuring methods, and examples discussed in this book are illustrative and educational in nature. They are intended to demonstrate concepts related to bank statement mortgage loan qualification and structuring, including deposit analysis, expense ratio application, and investor guideline

First Edition, 2026

Table of Contents

Introduction 6

Chapter 1: Understanding Personal Bank Statement Mortgage Loans and How Lenders Analyze Deposits.............................12

Chapter 2: Mastering Deposit Analysis for Personal Bank Statement Mortgage Loans..20

Chapter 3: Expense Factor Assumptions and How They Impact Your Qualifying Income...29

Chapter 4: Structuring Clean Personal Bank Accounts for Maximum Mortgage Approval..37

Chapter 5: Avoiding Red Flags and Strengthening Your Personal Bank Statement Loan File.......................................45

Chapter 6: Documentation Strategies to Maximize Income and Strengthen Approval..53

Chapter 7: Choosing the Right 12-Month vs. 24-Month Bank Statement Strategy...60

Chapter 8: Qualifying for Larger Loan Amounts and Scaling Your Borrowing Power..67

Chapter 9: Getting Approved with Credit Challenges Using Personal Bank Statements...74

Chapter 10: Advanced Bank Statement Loan Structuring – Engineering Approvals Using Deposits, Expense Ratios, and Investor Guidelines.......... 81

Chapter 11: Pre-Approval, Underwriting, and Closing – Navigating the Bank Statement Loan Process Step by Step... 89

Chapter 12: Long-Term Strategy – Using Personal Bank Statement Loans to Build Wealth and Financial Freedom..... 96

Chapter 13: Common Mistakes to Avoid and How to Protect Your Loan Approval.......... 103

Chapter 14:. Creating a Repeatable System – Turning Bank Statement Loans into a Scalable Financial Machine............. 110

Chapter 15: Final Strategy – From Loan Approval to Financial Independence Using Bank Statement Loans..........117

Final Thoughts..........124

Introduction

In today's evolving mortgage landscape, the traditional path to homeownership no longer fits everyone. For decades, borrowers were expected to prove their income through W-2s, pay stubs, and tax returns that neatly reflected a stable, predictable salary. But the modern workforce has shifted. Entrepreneurs, freelancers, consultants, real estate agents, content creators, and independent contractors now make up a rapidly growing portion of the economy. These individuals often earn substantial income, yet their financial profiles do not translate cleanly onto tax returns. Deductions, write-offs, and variable income streams frequently reduce taxable income on paper, even when actual cash flow is strong and consistent. This disconnect has historically created a major barrier to mortgage approval. Personal bank statement mortgage loans were designed to bridge that gap.

This book is dedicated to helping you understand how to qualify for a mortgage using your personal bank statements instead of traditional income documents. It is built specifically for borrowers who earn income outside the conventional W-2 structure and need a smarter, more flexible way to demonstrate their ability to repay a loan. Whether you are self-employed, paid on a 1099 basis, or operating a business that generates income flowing directly into your personal accounts, this strategy can open doors that may have previously seemed closed.

At the core of personal bank statement lending is a simple but powerful concept: cash flow tells the real story. Instead of relying on tax returns that may minimize income for tax purposes, lenders analyze deposits into your personal bank accounts over a defined period—typically 12 or 24 months—to determine your qualifying income. This approach allows lenders to evaluate what you actually earn and how consistently you earn it. It shifts the focus from reported income to real-world financial activity, giving borrowers a more accurate and often more favorable representation of their financial strength.

However, while this method offers flexibility, it is not without structure. Personal bank statement loans follow specific guidelines, and understanding these guidelines is the key to success. One of the most important aspects is deposit analysis. Not all deposits are treated equally. Lenders carefully review your bank statements to identify which deposits qualify as income and which do not. For example, consistent deposits from your business activities or client payments are typically counted, while transfers between accounts, one-time deposits, or non-recurring sources may be excluded. The goal is to establish a stable and reliable income pattern that supports your ability to repay the mortgage.

Another critical component is the application of expense factors. Since personal bank statements do not always clearly separate business and personal expenses, lenders often apply an assumed expense ratio to your deposits. This percentage represents estimated business expenses and is subtracted from your total deposits to arrive at your qualifying income. The exact percentage can vary depending on the lender, the industry you are in, and whether additional documentation—such as a profit and loss statement prepared by a CPA—is provided. Understanding how these expense factors work can significantly impact your loan approval and the amount you qualify for.

Equally important is how you structure your personal bank accounts. Clean, organized financial records can make the difference between a smooth approval and a complicated underwriting process. Lenders prefer to see consistent deposit patterns, minimal commingling of funds, and a clear separation between income and non-income transactions. While it is not always possible to achieve perfect separation, especially for self-employed individuals, there are strategic ways to present your finances that strengthen your application. Throughout this book, you will learn how to structure your accounts in a way that aligns with lender expectations and maximizes your qualifying income.

This introduction sets the stage for a deeper exploration of the strategies, principles, and techniques that define personal bank statement mortgage loans. In the chapters that follow, you will gain a step-by-step understanding of how lenders analyze your financial profile, how to prepare your documentation, and how to avoid common pitfalls that can delay or derail your approval. You will also learn how to position yourself as a strong borrower, even if your financial situation does not fit within traditional guidelines.

One of the most empowering aspects of this loan type is that it rewards consistency and clarity. Unlike traditional loans that rely heavily on static documents, personal bank statement loans evaluate your financial behavior over time. This means that every deposit, every transaction, and every pattern in your accounts contributes to your overall profile. By understanding how these elements are interpreted by underwriters, you can take control of your financial presentation and actively improve your chances of approval.

It is also important to recognize that this loan strategy is not just about getting approved—it is about building long-term financial flexibility. When you learn how to document your income effectively using bank statements, you gain the ability to navigate future lending opportunities with confidence. Whether you are purchasing a primary residence, refinancing an existing property, or expanding into real estate investing, the principles outlined in this book will continue to serve you.

As you move forward, keep in mind that every borrower's situation is unique. There is no one-size-fits-all approach, and success often comes down to understanding how to apply general guidelines to your specific circumstances. This book is designed to give you both the foundational knowledge and the practical strategies needed to do exactly that. It will help you see your finances through the lens of an underwriter, identify areas for improvement, and present your income in the strongest possible way.

You are entering a space where traditional limitations no longer define your options. Personal bank statement mortgage loans represent a shift toward more inclusive and realistic lending practices—ones that recognize the diversity of modern income streams and the value of real-world cash flow. By mastering the concepts in this book, you position yourself to take full advantage of these opportunities and move closer to your financial and homeownership goals.

This journey begins with understanding how your deposits tell your story. Every dollar that flows into your account has the potential to contribute to your approval when properly documented and presented. The key is knowing how to translate that flow into a clear, consistent, and compelling income narrative. That is exactly what this book will teach you to do.

Chapter 1

Understanding Personal Bank Statement Mortgage Loans and How Lenders Analyze Deposits

Personal bank statement mortgage loans represent one of the most powerful and practical solutions for borrowers whose income does not fit neatly into traditional lending guidelines. In this chapter, you will gain a deep understanding of how these loans work specifically when using personal bank statements, how lenders interpret deposits, and how you can strategically position your finances to qualify. This is not just about knowing the rules—it is about understanding how to use those rules to your advantage so you can confidently move forward in the mortgage process.

At the foundation of personal bank statement lending is the concept of cash flow-based income qualification. Instead of relying on tax returns, which often show reduced income due to deductions and write-offs, lenders evaluate the actual deposits that flow into your personal bank accounts. These deposits are used as a proxy for income, allowing lenders to determine your ability to repay the loan based on real financial activity rather than reported taxable income. This shift is especially important for self-employed individuals, freelancers, and business owners who reinvest heavily into their businesses and therefore show lower income on paper.

However, not every deposit into your account counts as qualifying income. Lenders are highly focused on identifying consistent, recurring deposits that reflect legitimate earnings. For example, if you are a consultant receiving payments from clients, those deposits—if consistent and traceable—can be counted. On the other hand, transfers between your own accounts, one-time large deposits, or funds that cannot be clearly sourced are typically excluded. The goal is to establish a stable income pattern that demonstrates reliability over time. This is why lenders usually require 12 or 24 months of personal bank statements. The longer the history, the more confidence the lender has in the consistency of your income.

One of the most critical aspects of deposit analysis is pattern recognition. Underwriters are trained to look for trends, not just totals. They examine whether deposits occur regularly, whether they are increasing, decreasing, or fluctuating, and whether there are any gaps that might indicate instability. For example, a borrower who deposits $8,000 to $12,000 consistently every month over 24 months will be viewed more favorably than someone who has sporadic deposits ranging from $2,000 to $20,000 with no clear pattern. Stability is often more important than peak income levels because it directly relates to your ability to make consistent mortgage payments.

Another key factor is the documentation and explanation of deposits. While personal bank statement loans are more flexible than traditional loans, they still require clarity. Lenders may ask for letters of explanation for certain deposits, especially if they are large or irregular. Being proactive in documenting your income sources can significantly streamline the process. For example, if you regularly receive payments from multiple clients, maintaining records such as invoices, contracts, or payment summaries can help support your deposit history and reduce the likelihood of delays during underwriting.

Expense factors also play a central role in determining your qualifying income. Because personal bank statements do not always clearly separate business expenses from personal expenses, lenders apply an assumed expense ratio to your deposits. This percentage is subtracted from your total deposits to estimate your net income. For instance, if a lender applies a 50 percent expense factor, only half of your deposits will be considered as qualifying income. Some borrowers may be able to reduce this percentage by providing additional documentation, such as a CPA-prepared profit and loss statement, which demonstrates lower actual expenses. Understanding how expense factors are applied—and how to influence them—can significantly impact the loan amount you qualify for.

Equally important is the concept of "clean" bank statements. Clean statements are those that clearly reflect income without excessive commingling, unexplained deposits, or irregular activity. While many self-employed borrowers use their personal accounts for both business and personal transactions, excessive mixing of funds can complicate the analysis and reduce the amount of income that can be counted. For example, frequent transfers between accounts, cash deposits without clear documentation, or large non-income deposits can raise red flags. By organizing your accounts and minimizing unnecessary complexity, you can present a stronger financial profile to the lender.

Consistency in banking behavior is another factor that lenders evaluate closely. This includes maintaining stable balances, avoiding overdrafts, and demonstrating responsible account management. While personal bank statement loans are designed for flexibility, lenders still want to see that you manage your finances responsibly. A history of overdrafts or negative balances can undermine an otherwise strong deposit profile, as it may indicate cash flow issues. On the other hand, maintaining healthy balances and consistent activity can serve as a compensating factor that strengthens your application.

As you begin to understand how lenders analyze personal bank statements, it becomes clear that preparation is everything. This is not a passive process where you simply submit your documents and hope for approval. Instead, it is an active strategy where you shape your financial presentation in a way that aligns with underwriting guidelines. By organizing your deposits, documenting your income sources, and minimizing unnecessary complexity, you can significantly improve your chances of approval and potentially qualify for better loan terms.

This chapter lays the groundwork for everything that follows in this book. The principles you have learned here—deposit analysis, expense factors, consistency, and account structuring—will be applied in increasingly advanced ways as you move forward. Each concept builds on the last, giving you a comprehensive understanding of how to navigate the personal bank statement loan process from start to finish.

Ultimately, personal bank statement mortgage loans are about telling your financial story in a way that lenders can understand and trust. Your bank statements are not just documents; they are a reflection of your income, your habits, and your financial stability. When presented correctly, they can open doors that traditional income documentation cannot. This is your opportunity to take control of that narrative and position yourself for success.

Real-Life Math Example: How a Borrower Qualifies Using Personal Bank Statements

To fully understand how personal bank statement mortgage loans work in practice, let's walk through a detailed real-life scenario. Imagine a borrower named Maria, who is a self-employed marketing consultant. Maria does not receive a W-2 salary. Instead, she works with multiple clients and receives payments directly into her personal bank account. Over the past two years, she has built a stable business and is now looking to purchase a home.

Maria provides 24 months of personal bank statements to her lender. After reviewing the statements, the lender identifies all qualifying deposits. Over the 24-month period, Maria has total deposits of $240,000. This averages to $10,000 per month in gross deposits. At first glance, this appears to be a strong income profile. However, the lender must apply an expense factor to determine Maria's qualifying income.

In Maria's case, the lender applies a standard 50 percent expense ratio because she has not provided a CPA-prepared profit and loss statement. This means that half of her deposits are assumed to be business expenses. As a result, her qualifying income is reduced from $10,000 per month to $5,000 per month. This figure is what the lender will use to determine how much mortgage Maria can afford.

Next, the lender evaluates Maria's debt obligations. She has a car payment of $500 per month, a student loan payment of $300 per month, and credit card minimum payments totaling $200 per month. This brings her total monthly debt obligations to $1,000. The lender then calculates her debt-to-income ratio using her qualifying income of $5,000. Her existing debts represent 20 percent of her income, leaving room for a mortgage payment within the lender's guidelines.

Assuming the lender allows a maximum debt-to-income ratio of 50 percent, Maria can allocate up to $2,500 per month toward her total housing payment, including principal, interest, taxes, and insurance. Based on current interest rates and loan terms, this could translate to a loan amount of approximately $400,000 to $450,000, depending on factors such as her credit score, down payment, and property taxes.

Now let's consider how Maria could improve her situation. If she had provided a CPA-prepared profit and loss statement showing that her actual expenses were only 30 percent of her income, the lender might have used a 30 percent expense factor instead of 50 percent. In that case, her qualifying income would increase from $5,000 per month to $7,000 per month. This higher income would significantly increase her borrowing power, potentially allowing her to qualify for a loan amount closer to $550,000 or more.

Additionally, if Maria had structured her bank accounts more strategically—such as separating business and personal transactions—she might have been able to present a cleaner financial profile. This could reduce underwriting questions and further strengthen her application. Even small improvements in how deposits are documented and categorized can have a meaningful impact on the final outcome.

This example illustrates the importance of understanding how lenders analyze personal bank statements and how different variables affect your qualifying income. It is not just about how much money you make—it is about how that income is presented, documented, and interpreted. By mastering these concepts, you can take control of the process and position yourself to achieve the best possible results.

As you move forward in this book, you will learn how to apply these strategies to your own situation, optimize your financial profile, and navigate the loan process with confidence.

Chapter 2

Mastering Deposit Analysis for Personal Bank Statement Mortgage Loans

Deposit analysis is the heart of personal bank statement mortgage lending. It is the single most important factor that determines how much income you can use to qualify and, ultimately, how much home you can afford. While many borrowers assume that all deposits into their account automatically count as income, the reality is far more nuanced. Lenders apply a detailed, methodical process to evaluate deposits, identify patterns, and determine which funds are stable, recurring, and eligible to be used for qualification. Understanding this process gives you a significant advantage and allows you to take control of your financial presentation before your loan even reaches underwriting.

At its core, deposit analysis is about distinguishing between true income and non-qualifying funds. Lenders are not simply adding up your deposits—they are interpreting them. They are looking for evidence that your income is consistent, reliable, and likely to continue in the future. This means that deposits must meet certain criteria to be counted. First, they must be recurring. A single large deposit, even if substantial, does not carry the same weight as smaller deposits that occur regularly over time. Recurring deposits demonstrate stability, which is one of the most important factors in mortgage approval.

Second, deposits must be sourced and explainable. Lenders want to understand where your money is coming from. If you are a consultant, your deposits might come from client payments. If you are a freelancer, they might come from platforms or direct contracts. If you are in sales, they might include commissions. Regardless of the source, the key is that the deposits can be tied to your income-generating activity. Deposits that cannot be clearly sourced—such as random transfers, gifts, or cash deposits without documentation—are often excluded from the analysis. This is why maintaining records such as invoices, payment confirmations, or contracts can be incredibly valuable.

Another important element of deposit analysis is consistency in timing and amount. Lenders examine not just how much you deposit, but when you deposit it and how frequently. For example, a borrower who deposits $8,000 every month on a predictable schedule presents a stronger profile than someone who deposits $24,000 once every three months. Even though the total income may be the same, the consistency of monthly deposits provides greater assurance that the borrower can handle a monthly mortgage payment. Predictability reduces perceived risk, and in lending, reduced risk often translates into better approval outcomes.

Seasonality is another factor that lenders take into account. Some borrowers have income that fluctuates throughout the year due to the nature of their business. For example, a real estate agent may earn more during peak selling seasons, while a contractor may have higher income during certain months. Lenders understand this and will often average income over a 12- or 24-month period to account for these fluctuations. However, large swings in income can still raise concerns, especially if there are periods with little or no deposits. The goal is to demonstrate that, even with fluctuations, your overall income remains stable and sufficient.

One of the most common challenges in deposit analysis is commingling of funds. This occurs when business and personal transactions are mixed within the same account. While this is common among self-employed individuals, it can make it more difficult for lenders to identify qualifying income. For example, if your account includes business revenue, personal transfers, loan proceeds, and other non-income deposits, the lender must carefully separate these elements to determine what counts. Excessive commingling can lead to more deposits being excluded, reducing your qualifying income. By minimizing unnecessary transfers and keeping your deposits as clean and straightforward as possible, you can improve your financial presentation.

Lenders also pay close attention to large or irregular deposits. These are deposits that fall outside your normal pattern and may require additional documentation. For example, if you typically deposit $5,000 to $7,000 per month and suddenly deposit $25,000, the lender will likely ask for an explanation. If that deposit is from a legitimate source—such as a large client payment—and can be documented, it may still be counted. However, if it cannot be clearly explained, it may be excluded. The key is not to avoid large deposits, but to ensure that they are properly documented and consistent with your business activity.

Another critical aspect of deposit analysis is averaging. Once the lender has identified all qualifying deposits, they calculate your average monthly income over the selected period. This is typically done by adding up all qualifying deposits and dividing by the number of months in the analysis period. The resulting figure becomes your gross monthly income before expense factors are applied. This averaging process smooths out fluctuations and provides a more accurate representation of your earning capacity.

It is also important to understand that lenders may choose between a 12-month and a 24-month analysis depending on your situation. A 24-month analysis provides a longer history and may be more favorable if your income has been stable or increasing over time. A 12-month analysis, on the other hand, may be beneficial if your income has recently increased and you want to highlight your current earning level. Choosing the right timeframe can have a significant impact on your qualifying income, and it is often a strategic decision made in collaboration with your loan officer.

As you can see, deposit analysis is not just a technical process—it is a strategic one. Every deposit you make, every transaction you record, and every pattern you establish contributes to your overall financial profile. By understanding how lenders interpret these elements, you can proactively shape your bank statements in a way that supports your loan application. This means being intentional about how you receive payments, how you manage your accounts, and how you document your income.

This chapter is about giving you the tools to take control of that process. When you understand deposit analysis at this level, you are no longer reacting to underwriting decisions—you are influencing them. You are presenting your income in the strongest possible light, reducing uncertainty, and increasing your chances of approval. This is one of the most powerful skills you can develop in the world of alternative mortgage financing.

Real-Life Math Example: Detailed Deposit Analysis and Income Calculation

Let's walk through a detailed real-life example to see how deposit analysis works step by step. Imagine a borrower named David, who is a self-employed fitness coach and online trainer. David receives payments from clients through various methods, including direct transfers, online platforms, and occasional cash deposits that he deposits into his personal bank account. He is applying for a mortgage using 12 months of personal bank statements.

Over the 12-month period, David's total deposits are $180,000. At first glance, this averages to $15,000 per month. However, the lender cannot simply use this number. Instead, they must analyze each deposit to determine which ones qualify as income.

After reviewing the statements, the lender identifies that $30,000 of the total deposits are transfers from David's savings account and other personal accounts. These are not considered income because they are simply movements of money he already owns. This reduces the total qualifying deposits to $150,000. Next, the lender identifies $10,000 in irregular deposits that cannot be clearly sourced or documented. These deposits are excluded as well, bringing the total qualifying deposits down to $140,000. Now, the lender divides $140,000 by 12 months to calculate David's average monthly gross income. This results in approximately $11,667 per month. This is the starting point for determining his qualifying income. However, the process is not complete yet, because the lender must apply an expense factor.

In David's case, the lender applies a 40 percent expense ratio based on his industry and the documentation he has provided. This means that 40 percent of his deposits are assumed to be business expenses. To calculate his net qualifying income, the lender multiplies $11,667 by 60 percent (the remaining portion after expenses). This results in a qualifying income of approximately $7,000 per month.

Next, the lender evaluates David's debts. He has a car payment of $400, credit card payments totaling $300, and a personal loan payment of $300, for a total of $1,000 in monthly debt obligations. Using his qualifying income of $7,000, his current debt-to-income ratio is approximately 14 percent. If the lender allows a maximum ratio of 50 percent, David can allocate up to $3,500 per month toward his housing payment.

Based on current interest rates and loan terms, this monthly housing allowance could translate to a loan amount of approximately $500,000 to $600,000, depending on factors such as down payment and property taxes. This demonstrates how deposit analysis directly impacts borrowing power.

Now let's consider how David could improve his outcome. If he had separated his accounts and avoided transferring funds between them, the $30,000 in excluded transfers might not have been an issue. Additionally, if he had documented the $10,000 in irregular deposits, some or all of that amount might have been included. This could increase his qualifying deposits to $170,000, raising his average monthly income and ultimately increasing his loan eligibility.

Furthermore, if David had provided a CPA-prepared profit and loss statement showing that his actual expenses were only 25 percent, the lender might have used a lower expense ratio. This would increase his qualifying income from $7,000 to approximately $8,750 per month, significantly boosting his purchasing power.

This example highlights the importance of every detail in deposit analysis. Small adjustments in documentation, account structure, and expense verification can lead to substantial differences in qualifying income. By understanding and applying these principles, you can maximize your financial profile and achieve better outcomes in the mortgage process.

As you continue through this book, you will build on this knowledge and learn how to refine your strategy even further. Deposit analysis is not just a requirement—it is an opportunity to present your income in the most effective way possible.

Chapter 3

Expense Factor Assumptions and How They Impact Your Qualifying Income

One of the most misunderstood yet powerful components of personal bank statement mortgage loans is the expense factor. While deposit analysis determines your gross income based on the money flowing into your account, the expense factor determines how much of that income you are actually allowed to use to qualify. This single percentage can dramatically increase or decrease your borrowing power, making it one of the most critical variables in the entire approval process. Understanding how expense factors work—and how to influence them—can be the difference between qualifying for your ideal home or falling short of your goals.

At a basic level, the expense factor represents an estimate of your business expenses. Because personal bank statements do not always clearly separate business-related costs from personal spending, lenders apply a standardized percentage to your deposits to account for expenses. This allows them to approximate your net income without requiring full tax returns. For example, if you have $10,000 in average monthly deposits and the lender applies a 50 percent expense factor, only $5,000 will be considered qualifying income. The remaining $5,000 is assumed to cover business expenses such as materials, marketing, travel, or operational costs.

However, this percentage is not arbitrary. It is based on a combination of lender guidelines, industry standards, and the level of documentation you provide. Different industries have different expense profiles. For example, a consultant or coach who operates primarily online may have lower expenses compared to a contractor who incurs costs for materials, labor, and equipment. As a result, lenders may apply lower expense factors to low-overhead businesses and higher factors to industries with significant operating costs. Understanding where your business falls within this spectrum can help you anticipate how your income will be evaluated.

One of the most important concepts to understand is that the default expense factor is often conservative. Many lenders will start with a standard assumption—commonly around 50 percent—unless additional documentation is provided to justify a lower percentage. This means that, without proper preparation, you may be qualifying with only half of your actual income. For many borrowers, this is a major missed opportunity. By taking steps to document your true expenses, you can potentially reduce the expense factor and significantly increase your qualifying income. The most effective way to influence your expense factor is through a CPA-prepared profit and loss statement. This document provides a detailed breakdown of your business income and expenses, offering lenders a more accurate picture of your financial situation. If your actual expenses are lower than the standard assumption, the lender may use your documented expense ratio instead of the default percentage. For example, if your CPA-prepared statement shows that your expenses are only 30 percent of your income, the lender may use a 30 percent expense factor instead of 50 percent. This adjustment can have a profound impact on your loan eligibility.

Another strategy for improving your expense factor is to maintain clean and organized financial records. Even without a CPA-prepared statement, borrowers who can clearly demonstrate their income and expense patterns may be able to negotiate a more favorable ratio. This includes maintaining consistent deposits, minimizing commingling of funds, and avoiding excessive or unexplained transactions. The clearer your financial picture, the more confidence the lender has in applying a lower expense factor.

It is also important to understand how expense factors interact with other aspects of the loan process. For example, your qualifying income—after expenses—is used to calculate your debt-to-income ratio. This ratio determines how much of your income can be allocated toward your mortgage payment. A higher qualifying income allows for a higher allowable payment, which in turn increases your borrowing capacity. This means that even a small reduction in your expense factor can lead to a significant increase in the loan amount you qualify for.

Timing can also play a role in how expense factors are applied. If your business has recently become more efficient or profitable, your most recent financial data may show lower expenses compared to earlier periods. In such cases, using a 12-month analysis instead of a 24-month analysis may allow you to highlight your improved financial performance. This is another example of how strategic planning can influence your outcome.

Another key consideration is the trade-off between simplicity and optimization. While it may be easier to rely on the lender's default expense factor, doing so often results in a lower qualifying income. On the other hand, providing additional documentation—such as a CPA-prepared statement—requires more effort but can lead to a much stronger application. Understanding this trade-off allows you to make informed decisions about how much time and effort to invest in preparing your loan file.

It is also worth noting that expense factors are not just about approval—they are about sustainability. By accurately accounting for your expenses, lenders are ensuring that you can realistically afford your mortgage payment. This protects both you and the lender from financial strain. While it may be tempting to minimize expenses to maximize your qualifying income, it is important to strike a balance that reflects your true financial situation.

As you move forward, think of the expense factor as a lever that you can control. By understanding how it works and taking steps to influence it, you can significantly improve your financial profile. This chapter is not just about understanding a percentage—it is about recognizing the power behind that percentage and using it to your advantage.

Real-Life Math Example: How Expense Factors Transform Borrowing Power

Now, we're going to walk through a detailed real-life scenario to illustrate how expense factors impact qualifying income and loan eligibility. Imagine a borrower named Alex, who is a self-employed graphic designer. Alex receives payments from clients directly into his personal bank account and is applying for a mortgage using 24 months of personal bank statements.

Over the 24-month period, Alex has total qualifying deposits of $360,000. This averages to $15,000 per month in gross income. At first glance, this appears to position Alex as a strong borrower. However, the lender must apply an expense factor to determine his net qualifying income.

In the first scenario, Alex does not provide any additional documentation, so the lender applies a standard 50 percent expense factor. This reduces his qualifying income from $15,000 per month to $7,500 per month. The lender then evaluates his debts, which total $1,500 per month. This results in a debt-to-income ratio of 20 percent before adding a mortgage payment. Assuming the lender allows a maximum ratio of 50 percent, Alex can allocate up to $3,750 per month toward housing.

Based on current interest rates, this monthly payment might support a loan amount of approximately $550,000. While this is a solid approval, it does not fully reflect Alex's true earning potential.

Now let's consider a second scenario. Alex works with a CPA to prepare a detailed profit and loss statement showing that his actual business expenses are only 30 percent of his income. With this documentation, the lender agrees to use a 30 percent expense factor instead of 50 percent. This increases Alex's qualifying income from $7,500 to $10,500 per month.

With the same $1,500 in monthly debts, his debt-to-income ratio drops to approximately 14 percent before housing. This allows him to allocate up to $5,250 per month toward his mortgage. At this higher payment level, Alex may now qualify for a loan amount closer to $750,000 or more, depending on other factors.

The difference between these two scenarios is significant. By reducing the expense factor from 50 percent to 30 percent, Alex increases his qualifying income by $3,000 per month and his potential loan amount by approximately $200,000. This demonstrates the powerful impact that expense factors can have on borrowing capacity.

Now let's take it one step further. Suppose Alex also improves his financial presentation by separating his business and personal accounts, eliminating unnecessary transfers, and documenting all deposits clearly. This strengthens his overall profile and may allow the lender to apply even more favorable terms, such as a slightly higher allowable debt-to-income ratio or better interest rates.

This example highlights a key principle: your qualifying income is not fixed—it is influenced by how your finances are presented and documented. By understanding and optimizing expense factors, you can unlock additional borrowing power and achieve better outcomes in the mortgage process. As you continue through this book, you will learn how to combine this knowledge with other strategies to create a comprehensive approach to personal bank statement lending. The goal is not just to qualify, but to qualify in the strongest possible way.

Chapter 4

Structuring Clean Personal Bank Accounts for Maximum Mortgage Approval

When it comes to personal bank statement mortgage loans, how you manage your bank accounts can be just as important as how much money you earn. Many borrowers focus solely on increasing income, but overlook the structure and presentation of their financial activity. In reality, lenders are not only evaluating how much you deposit—they are evaluating how clearly and consistently your deposits tell a reliable income story. A clean, well-structured bank account can significantly increase your qualifying income, reduce underwriting conditions, and speed up approval. On the other hand, a disorganized account filled with transfers, unexplained deposits, and inconsistent activity can reduce your usable income and create unnecessary obstacles.

At the core of account structuring is clarity. Lenders want to easily identify which deposits represent income and which do not. The simpler and more transparent your account activity is, the easier it is for an underwriter to approve your file. This means reducing noise in your bank statements. Noise includes excessive transfers between accounts, frequent movement of money that does not represent income, and deposits that cannot be easily explained. While these activities may be normal in your day-to-day financial life, they can complicate the underwriting process and lead to more deposits being excluded from your qualifying income.

One of the most effective strategies for creating clean bank statements is minimizing commingling. Commingling occurs when business and personal funds are mixed within the same account. While this is common for self-employed individuals, it makes it more difficult for lenders to distinguish income from non-income transactions. Ideally, income should flow into a primary account in a consistent and predictable manner, without unnecessary transfers or mixing. Even if you continue to use a personal account for business income, being intentional about how deposits are made can make a significant difference.

Consistency is another critical factor. Lenders are looking for patterns that demonstrate stability. This includes consistent deposit amounts, consistent timing, and consistent sources. For example, if you receive payments from clients, it is beneficial to deposit those payments in a regular manner rather than in large, irregular batches. Consistency helps build a clear narrative that your income is ongoing and reliable.

Even if your income fluctuates, maintaining a structured deposit pattern can improve how it is perceived during underwriting.

Another important aspect of account structuring is avoiding unnecessary transfers. Transfers between your own accounts do not count as income, and excessive transfers can create confusion. For example, if you move money from one account to another and then deposit it again, it may appear as additional income unless clearly identified. This can lead to delays, additional documentation requests, or even exclusion of certain deposits. By limiting transfers and keeping your income deposits separate from internal movements, you can present a cleaner financial picture.

Cash deposits require special attention. While cash income is common in certain industries, it can be more difficult to document and verify. Lenders may be cautious when evaluating cash deposits, especially if they are large or inconsistent. If you regularly receive cash payments, it is important to establish a consistent pattern and maintain records that support the source of those funds. Without proper documentation, cash deposits may be excluded from your qualifying income, reducing your borrowing power.

Another key strategy is maintaining strong average balances.

While deposit analysis focuses on income, lenders also consider your overall financial stability. Consistently maintaining a healthy balance in your account can serve as a compensating factor, demonstrating that you manage your finances responsibly and have reserves available. This can strengthen your application and provide additional confidence to the lender.

Timing also plays a role in account structuring. Preparing your bank statements is not something that should begin when you decide to apply for a mortgage—it should start months in advance. By being proactive, you can create a consistent and organized financial history that aligns with lender expectations. This includes planning your deposits, reducing unnecessary transactions, and ensuring that your account activity reflects your true income in the clearest possible way.

It is also important to think of your bank statements as a story. Every transaction contributes to the narrative that an underwriter will interpret. Your goal is to present a story of stability, consistency, and transparency. This means eliminating confusion, documenting your income sources, and maintaining a clean and organized account structure. When your bank statements tell a clear story, the underwriting process becomes smoother and more predictable.

Another often overlooked factor is the psychological aspect of underwriting. While guidelines and formulas play a major role, underwriters are also human. A clean, well-organized file creates confidence and makes it easier for them to approve your loan. Conversely, a messy or confusing file can lead to hesitation, additional scrutiny, and more conditions. By presenting your finances in a clear and professional manner, you are not only meeting the guidelines—you are making it easier for the underwriter to say yes.

As you move forward, remember that structuring your bank accounts is not about changing your income—it is about changing how your income is presented. Small adjustments in how you manage your accounts can lead to significant improvements in your qualifying income and overall loan outcome. This chapter is about giving you the awareness and strategies needed to take control of that process.

Real-Life Math Example: How Account Structure Impacts Qualifying Income

Let's walk through a detailed real-life example to illustrate how structuring your bank accounts can directly impact your qualifying income and loan approval. Imagine a borrower named Sophia, who is a self-employed event planner. Sophia earns a strong income, but her financial activity is spread across multiple accounts, with frequent transfers and mixed transactions. Over a 12-month period, Sophia's personal bank statements show total deposits of $240,000, which averages to $20,000 per month. At first glance, this appears to position her as a high-income borrower. However, the lender must analyze her deposits carefully to determine which ones qualify as income.

After reviewing her statements, the lender identifies that $60,000 of the deposits are transfers from other accounts she owns. These transfers do not count as income because they are simply movements of existing funds. This reduces her qualifying deposits to $180,000. Next, the lender identifies $20,000 in deposits that cannot be clearly sourced due to inconsistent descriptions and lack of documentation. These deposits are excluded as well, bringing her total qualifying deposits down to $160,000.

Now, the lender divides $160,000 by 12 months to calculate her average monthly income, resulting in approximately $13,333 per month. This is significantly lower than the original $20,000 average suggested by her total deposits. Next, the lender applies a 50 percent expense factor, reducing her qualifying income to approximately $6,667 per month.

With this income, Sophia may qualify for a loan amount of around $450,000 to $500,000, depending on her debts and other factors. However, this does not reflect her true earning potential—it reflects how her income is presented. Now let's consider a second scenario where Sophia restructures her accounts. She begins depositing all client payments into a single primary account, avoids transferring funds between accounts unnecessarily, and documents all income sources clearly. Over the next 12 months, her total deposits remain the same at $240,000, but her account activity is much cleaner.

In this improved scenario, the lender is able to count $220,000 of her deposits as qualifying income, excluding only a small portion for minor transfers. This results in an average monthly income of approximately $18,333. After applying the same 50 percent expense factor, her qualifying income increases to approximately $9,167 per month.

With this higher income, Sophia can now qualify for a loan amount closer to $650,000 or more. This represents an increase of over $150,000 in borrowing power, achieved without increasing her actual income—only by improving how it is structured and presented.

Now let's take it one step further. If Sophia also provides a CPA-prepared profit and loss statement showing that her actual expenses are only 30 percent, her qualifying income increases even further. Applying a 30 percent expense factor to

$18,333 results in a qualifying income of approximately $12,833 per month. This could allow her to qualify for a loan amount exceeding $800,000, depending on other factors.

This example demonstrates the powerful impact of account structuring. The same income can produce vastly different outcomes depending on how it is presented. By eliminating unnecessary transfers, documenting deposits, and maintaining a clean financial profile, borrowers can significantly increase their qualifying income and improve their loan options.

As you continue through this book, you will build on these strategies and learn how to optimize every aspect of your financial presentation. The goal is not just to qualify, but to qualify at your highest potential.

Chapter 5

Avoiding Red Flags and Strengthening Your Personal Bank Statement Loan File

In the world of personal bank statement mortgage loans, success is not only about what you do right—it is also about what you avoid doing wrong. Many borrowers with strong income and solid financial backgrounds are delayed, reduced, or even denied simply because their bank statements raise concerns during underwriting. These concerns, often referred to as red flags, do not necessarily mean that a borrower is unqualified. Instead, they create uncertainty. And in lending, uncertainty leads to caution. This chapter is designed to help you identify, understand, and eliminate those red flags so you can present a clean, confident, and approval-ready loan file.

A red flag is any pattern, transaction, or inconsistency in your financial profile that causes the underwriter to question the stability, legitimacy, or sustainability of your income. These can appear in many forms, and often they are unintentional. For example, frequent overdrafts may suggest cash flow instability. Large unexplained deposits may raise questions about income sourcing. Excessive transfers between accounts may create confusion about what is actual income. Each of these issues can reduce your qualifying income, trigger additional documentation requests, or delay the approval process.

One of the most common red flags is inconsistent deposit patterns. Lenders rely heavily on consistency to determine whether your income is stable. If your deposits vary significantly from month to month without a clear explanation, it can create doubt about your ability to maintain that income in the future. For example, if one month shows $20,000 in deposits and the next shows only $3,000, the lender may question whether your income is reliable. While some variation is expected—especially in self-employed income—extreme fluctuations should be explained and supported with documentation whenever possible.

Another major red flag is large, irregular deposits. These are deposits that fall outside your normal pattern and cannot be easily tied to your income-generating activity. For instance, if you typically deposit $8,000 per month and suddenly deposit $50,000, the lender will require an explanation. If that deposit is from a legitimate source—such as a large contract payment—and can be documented, it may still be counted. However, if it cannot be verified, it will likely be excluded and may raise broader concerns about the reliability of your income. Overdrafts and negative balances are also significant red flags. Even if your income is strong, a history of overdrafts suggests poor cash flow management. Lenders interpret this as a risk factor, as it indicates that you may struggle to manage monthly obligations. A single overdraft may not be critical, but repeated occurrences can weaken your file. Maintaining positive balances and avoiding overdrafts in the months leading up to your application is one of the simplest and most effective ways to strengthen your profile.

Commingling of funds, while common, can also become a red flag when it creates confusion. When business and personal transactions are heavily mixed, it becomes difficult for the lender to distinguish income from non-income activity. This can lead to more deposits being excluded or require additional documentation to clarify. While complete separation is not always necessary, reducing unnecessary mixing and maintaining a clear flow of income can significantly improve your file.

Unexplained cash deposits are another area of concern. Cash is inherently more difficult to document, and lenders are cautious when evaluating it. If cash deposits are consistent and supported by a clear business model—such as a service-based business that regularly receives cash payments—they may be considered. However, sporadic or large cash deposits without documentation are often excluded. If your business involves cash, it is essential to maintain records that clearly support the source of those funds.

Another subtle but important red flag is declining income. Lenders analyze trends over time, and a downward trend in deposits can indicate instability. For example, if your deposits decrease steadily over a 12- or 24-month period, the lender may question whether your income will continue at a sufficient level. In some cases, lenders may use the lower end of your income range or require additional documentation to confirm stability. If your income has declined for legitimate reasons, such as a temporary slowdown or a strategic business shift, providing context can help mitigate concerns.

Excessive account activity can also create challenges. While active accounts are normal, an unusually high volume of transactions—especially those that are not clearly related to income—can make it more difficult for underwriters to analyze your statements. Simplifying your account activity and reducing unnecessary transactions can make your file easier to review and more favorable in the eyes of the lender.

The key to avoiding red flags is preparation. By reviewing your bank statements before submitting them to a lender, you can identify potential issues and address them proactively. This may involve documenting certain deposits, restructuring your accounts, or simply waiting until your financial activity reflects a stronger and more consistent pattern. Taking control of this process allows you to present your finances in the best possible light.

It is also important to understand that red flags are not permanent obstacles—they are opportunities for improvement. Many issues can be resolved with proper documentation or by making adjustments to your financial behavior over time. The goal is not perfection, but clarity and consistency. When your bank statements tell a clear and reliable story, underwriters can focus on approving your loan rather than questioning your income.

This chapter is about empowering you to take control of your financial narrative. By recognizing and eliminating red flags, you reduce uncertainty, increase confidence, and position yourself for a smoother and more successful mortgage process.

Real-Life Math Example: How Red Flags Reduce Qualifying Income and How to Fix Them

Now, we're going to walk through a detailed real-life example to illustrate how red flags can impact your qualifying income and how addressing them can dramatically improve your outcome. Imagine a borrower named Daniel, who is a self-employed contractor applying for a mortgage using 12 months of personal bank statements.

Over the 12-month period, Daniel's total deposits are $300,000, which averages to $25,000 per month. At first glance, this suggests a very strong income profile. However, the lender must analyze the deposits to determine which ones qualify.

During the review, the lender identifies $80,000 in transfers between Daniel's personal and business accounts. These transfers do not count as income and are excluded. This reduces the total qualifying deposits to $220,000. Next, the lender identifies $40,000 in large, irregular deposits that cannot be clearly documented. These deposits are also excluded, bringing the total qualifying deposits down to $180,000.

Additionally, Daniel has several months with overdrafts and negative balances. While these do not directly reduce his income, they raise concerns about cash flow stability. As a result, the lender applies a more conservative approach when evaluating his file. They proceed with the remaining $180,000 in qualifying deposits, which averages to $15,000 per month.

The lender then applies a 50 percent expense factor, reducing Daniel's qualifying income to $7,500 per month. Based on this income, Daniel may qualify for a loan amount of approximately $550,000, depending on his debts and other factors. While this is still a viable approval, it is significantly lower than what his original deposit total suggested.

Now let's consider how Daniel could improve his situation. First, he restructures his accounts to eliminate unnecessary transfers. By keeping his income deposits in a single account and avoiding internal movements, he reduces the amount of excluded deposits. In the following year, his total deposits remain at $300,000, but only $20,000 are identified as transfers, increasing his qualifying deposits to $280,000.

Next, Daniel begins documenting his large deposits by maintaining invoices and contracts for each project. This allows the lender to verify an additional $30,000 that was previously excluded. His qualifying deposits now increase to $310,000, or approximately $25,833 per month.

He also improves his account management by maintaining positive balances and avoiding overdrafts. This strengthens his overall profile and increases the lender's confidence in his financial stability.

With these improvements, the lender calculates his average monthly income at $25,833. Applying the same 50 percent expense factor results in a qualifying income of approximately

$12,917 per month. This nearly doubles his previous qualifying income. With this higher income, Daniel can now qualify for a loan amount closer to $900,000 or more, depending on other factors. This represents an increase of over $300,000 in borrowing power, achieved not by increasing his income, but by eliminating red flags and improving how his finances are presented.

This example demonstrates a critical lesson: red flags do not just create inconvenience—they directly impact your qualifying income and loan outcome. By identifying and addressing these issues, you can unlock your full earning potential and significantly improve your mortgage options.

As you continue through this book, you will learn how to refine your strategy even further, combining clean account structuring, optimized expense factors, and strong documentation to create a powerful and approval-ready loan file.

Chapter 6

Documentation Strategies to Maximize Income and Strengthen Approval

In personal bank statement mortgage lending, documentation is not just a requirement—it is a powerful tool. While bank statements provide the foundation for qualifying income, the way you support and explain those statements can significantly influence how much of your income is accepted and how smoothly your loan moves through underwriting. Many borrowers mistakenly believe that bank statement loans require minimal documentation. While it is true that they are more flexible than traditional loans, the reality is that strategic documentation can dramatically improve your outcome. This chapter will show you how to use documentation not just to meet requirements, but to maximize your qualifying income and strengthen your approval.

At the core of documentation strategy is clarity. Lenders are not simply reviewing numbers—they are evaluating a story. Your job is to make that story as clear, consistent, and credible as possible. Every deposit, every fluctuation, and every pattern in your bank statements should be supported by documentation that explains and validates your income. When your file is clear, underwriters can move quickly and confidently. When it is unclear, they must pause, question, and request additional information, which can delay or weaken your approval.

One of the most powerful documents you can provide is a profit and loss statement, commonly referred to as a P&L. A CPA-prepared P&L carries significant weight because it provides a professional, third-party breakdown of your income and expenses. This document can be used to justify a lower expense factor, which directly increases your qualifying income. For example, if your bank statements show $15,000 per month in deposits and the lender would normally apply a 50 percent expense factor, a CPA-prepared P&L showing only 30 percent expenses could increase your qualifying income by thousands of dollars per month. This is one of the most effective ways to improve your borrowing power without changing your actual income.

Another key document is a letter of explanation, often referred to as an LOE. This is your opportunity to proactively address any potential concerns in your bank statements. For example, if you have a large deposit that falls outside your normal pattern, you can explain its source and provide supporting documentation. If your income fluctuates due to seasonal business cycles, you can outline that pattern and show how it averages out over time. A well-written letter of explanation can eliminate confusion and prevent delays, allowing the underwriter to focus on approving your loan rather than questioning your file.

Invoices and contracts are also valuable forms of documentation. These documents help establish the legitimacy and consistency of your income. For example, if you are a freelancer or consultant, providing invoices that match your bank deposits can strengthen your case. Contracts with clients can demonstrate ongoing business relationships, which supports the stability of your income. The goal is to create a clear connection between your income-generating activities and the deposits in your bank statements.

Business licenses and proof of operation are another important component. Lenders want to confirm that your business is legitimate and actively operating. Providing documentation such as a business license, website, or marketing materials can reinforce your credibility. This is especially important for borrowers who operate in less traditional industries or have recently started their business. The more evidence you provide of your business activity, the more confidence the lender has in your income.

Consistency between documents is critical. All of your documentation should align with your bank statements and tell the same story. For example, if your P&L shows a certain level of income, it should be consistent with the deposits in your bank statements. Any discrepancies can raise questions and lead to additional scrutiny. By ensuring that all of your documents are consistent and accurate, you create a cohesive and reliable financial profile.

Another important strategy is timing your documentation. Preparing your file in advance allows you to address potential issues before they become problems. For example, if you know that your bank statements include irregular deposits, you can gather documentation to support those deposits ahead of time. This proactive approach reduces the likelihood of delays and gives you greater control over the process.

It is also important to understand that more documentation is not always better. The goal is not to overwhelm the underwriter with information, but to provide the right information in a clear and organized manner. Quality matters more than quantity. Each document you provide should serve a purpose and contribute to a stronger, clearer file.

Documentation also plays a key role in mitigating risk. From the lender's perspective, every loan involves a level of uncertainty. By providing thorough and credible documentation, you reduce that uncertainty and increase the lender's confidence in your ability to repay the loan. This can lead to smoother approvals, fewer conditions, and potentially better loan terms.

As you move forward, think of documentation as a strategic advantage. It is not just about meeting requirements—it is about presenting your financial story in the most compelling way possible. When used effectively, documentation can transform your loan file from average to exceptional.

Real-Life Math Example: How Documentation Increases Qualifying Income and Loan Approval

Let's walk through a detailed real-life example to see how documentation can directly impact qualifying income and borrowing power. Imagine a borrower named Kevin, who is a self-employed digital marketing consultant applying for a mortgage using 24 months of personal bank statements.

Over the 24-month period, Kevin's total deposits are $480,000, which averages to $20,000 per month. Initially, the lender identifies $60,000 in transfers between accounts and excludes them, leaving $420,000 in qualifying deposits. This results in an average monthly income of $17,500.

Without additional documentation, the lender applies a standard 50 percent expense factor. This reduces Kevin's qualifying income to $8,750 per month. Based on this income,

Kevin may qualify for a loan amount of approximately $600,000 to $650,000, depending on his debts and other factors.

Now let's consider how documentation can improve his outcome. Kevin works with a CPA to prepare a detailed profit and loss statement showing that his actual business expenses are only 25 percent of his income. With this documentation, the lender agrees to use a 25 percent expense factor instead of 50 percent. This increases his qualifying income from $8,750 to approximately $13,125 per month.

Next, Kevin provides invoices and contracts that support an additional $30,000 in deposits that were initially excluded due to lack of documentation. This increases his qualifying deposits to $450,000, or approximately $18,750 per month. Applying the 25 percent expense factor results in a new qualifying income of approximately $14,063 per month.

Kevin also provides a letter of explanation for several large deposits, along with supporting documentation. This allows the lender to include an additional $20,000 in deposits, bringing his total qualifying deposits to $470,000. His average monthly income increases to approximately $19,583, and his qualifying income after expenses rises to approximately $14,687 per month. With this higher income, Kevin's borrowing power increases significantly. Instead of qualifying for a $600,000 loan, he may now qualify for a loan amount closer to $900,000 or more, depending on other factors. This represents an increase of over $250,000 in borrowing capacity, achieved through strategic documentation.

This example demonstrates that documentation is not just a formality—it is a powerful tool that can unlock additional income and improve your loan outcome. By providing clear, consistent, and credible documentation, you can maximize your qualifying income and position yourself for success in the mortgage process.

As you continue through this book, you will learn how to combine these documentation strategies with other techniques to create a comprehensive and highly effective loan application. The goal is to take full control of your financial presentation and achieve the best possible results.

Chapter 7

Choosing the Right 12-Month vs. 24-Month Bank Statement Strategy

One of the most strategic decisions you will make when applying for a personal bank statement mortgage loan is whether to use 12 months or 24 months of bank statements. While this may seem like a simple choice, it can have a significant impact on your qualifying income, your approval strength, and ultimately the loan amount you are able to secure. This chapter will help you understand how lenders evaluate each option, when to use one over the other, and how to position your financial profile to achieve the best possible outcome.

At a fundamental level, the difference between a 12-month and a 24-month bank statement program comes down to how your income is averaged. Lenders take your qualifying deposits over the selected period and divide them by the number of months to determine your average monthly income. This means that the timeframe you choose directly affects your calculated income. If your income has been stable or increasing, a shorter timeframe may highlight your strongest performance. If your income has been inconsistent or has declined recently, a longer timeframe may smooth out fluctuations and present a more stable average.

The 24-month option is often viewed as the more conservative and stable approach. By analyzing two full years of income, lenders gain a broader perspective on your financial history. This can be particularly beneficial if your income fluctuates seasonally or if you have experienced temporary dips. The longer timeframe allows high-performing months to offset lower-performing ones, resulting in a more balanced average. For borrowers with uneven income patterns, this can be the key to demonstrating consistency and qualifying successfully.

On the other hand, the 12-month option can be a powerful tool for borrowers whose income has recently increased. If your business has grown, your client base has expanded, or your pricing has improved, your most recent 12 months may reflect a significantly higher income than your 24-month average. In this case, using a 12-month analysis allows you to capture your current earning potential rather than being weighed down by earlier, lower-income periods. This can lead to a higher qualifying income and greater borrowing power.

However, the 12-month option also comes with higher scrutiny. Because it relies on a shorter history, lenders may require stronger consistency within that period. Large fluctuations, gaps in income, or irregular deposit patterns may be more closely examined. In some cases, lenders may require additional documentation or compensating factors to offset the shorter timeframe. This is why it is important to ensure that your most recent 12 months present a clear and stable income pattern before choosing this option.

Another key consideration is trend analysis. Lenders do not just calculate averages—they also evaluate whether your income is increasing, decreasing, or remaining stable. A positive trend can strengthen your application, while a negative trend can raise concerns. For example, if your income has steadily increased over the past two years, a 12-month analysis may highlight your upward trajectory. Conversely, if your income has declined recently, a 24-month analysis may help mitigate that decline by incorporating earlier, stronger months.

Expense factors also interact with the timeframe you choose. Because expense factors are applied to your average monthly income, a higher average income will result in a higher qualifying income after expenses. This means that choosing the right timeframe can amplify the benefits of a favorable expense factor. For example, if your 12-month average is significantly higher than your 24-month average, applying a lower expense factor to the 12-month income can dramatically increase your qualifying income.

It is also important to consider the stability of your business. If your business is well-established with consistent income over several years, a 24-month analysis may provide a strong and reliable profile. If your business is newer but growing rapidly, a 12-month analysis may better reflect your current reality. Understanding where you are in your business lifecycle can help guide your decision.

Another strategic factor is timing your application. If you anticipate that your income will continue to increase, it may be beneficial to wait until your most recent 12 months reflect that growth. Conversely, if you expect a temporary slowdown, applying sooner and using a 24-month average may help preserve a higher qualifying income. Timing is not just about when you apply—it is about when your financial profile is strongest.

It is also worth noting that some lenders may offer both options, while others may have specific requirements or preferences. Working with a knowledgeable loan officer can help you evaluate your options and determine which strategy aligns best with your financial situation. The goal is not just to qualify, but to qualify under the most favorable terms possible.

Ultimately, choosing between 12-month and 24-month bank statements is about control. It is about understanding how your income is evaluated and using that knowledge to your advantage. By analyzing your financial history, identifying trends, and strategically selecting the right timeframe, you can maximize your qualifying income and strengthen your loan application.

This chapter is about giving you that control. It is about helping you see your financial profile through the eyes of a lender and making decisions that position you for success.

Real-Life Math Example: Comparing 12-Month vs. 24-Month Income Qualification

Now, we're going to walk through a detailed real-life example to see how choosing between a 12-month and 24-month bank statement program can impact qualifying income and loan eligibility. Imagine a borrower named Lisa, who is a self-employed online business owner. Over the past two years, her business has grown significantly, with income increasing steadily.

In the first 12 months, Lisa's total deposits were $180,000, averaging $15,000 per month. In the most recent 12 months, her total deposits increased to $300,000, averaging $25,000 per month. Over the full 24-month period, her total deposits are $480,000, which averages to $20,000 per month.

If Lisa chooses the 24-month option, the lender will use the $20,000 monthly average as her gross income. After applying a 50 percent expense factor, her qualifying income becomes $10,000 per month. Based on this income, she may qualify for a loan amount of approximately $700,000, depending on her debts and other factors.

Now let's consider the 12-month option using her most recent income. With an average of $25,000 per month, applying the same 50 percent expense factor results in a qualifying income of $12,500 per month. This higher income could allow her to qualify for a loan amount closer to $875,000 or more.

The difference between these two options is substantial. By choosing the 12-month analysis, Lisa increases her qualifying income by $2,500 per month and her borrowing power by approximately $175,000. This demonstrates the importance of selecting the right timeframe based on your income trends.

Now let's take it one step further. Suppose Lisa provides a CPA-prepared profit and loss statement showing that her actual expenses are only 30 percent. Using the 24-month average of $20,000, her qualifying income would increase to

$14,000 per month. Using the 12-month average of $25,000, her qualifying income would increase to $17,500 per month.

With the higher income, her borrowing power increases even further. Under the 24-month scenario, she may qualify for a loan amount around $950,000. Under the 12-month scenario, she may qualify for a loan amount exceeding $1.2 million, depending on other factors.

This example highlights the combined impact of timeframe selection and expense factor optimization. By choosing the right timeframe and providing strong documentation, Lisa is able to significantly increase her qualifying income and loan eligibility.

However, it is important to consider potential risks. If Lisa's most recent 12 months included significant fluctuations or irregular deposits, the lender might scrutinize her file more closely or require additional documentation. In such cases, the 24-month option might provide a more stable and reliable profile, even if the average income is lower.

This example illustrates that there is no one-size-fits-all answer. The best choice depends on your unique financial situation, your income trends, and how your bank statements are structured. By understanding these variables and applying the strategies outlined in this chapter, you can make informed decisions that maximize your loan potential.

As you continue through this book, you will build on these concepts and learn how to integrate them into a comprehensive strategy for personal bank statement mortgage success.

Chapter 8

Qualifying for Larger Loan Amounts and Scaling Your Borrowing Power

As you progress through your understanding of personal bank statement mortgage loans, the focus naturally shifts from simply getting approved to maximizing how much you can qualify for. This chapter is about scaling—taking everything you have learned so far and applying it strategically to increase your borrowing power. Whether your goal is to purchase a higher-priced home, invest in real estate, or build long-term wealth, understanding how to qualify for larger loan amounts is essential.

At its core, borrowing power is driven by one primary factor: qualifying income. Every strategy you implement—cleaning up your bank statements, documenting your deposits, reducing your expense factor, and choosing the right timeframe—feeds into this number. The higher your qualifying income, the higher your allowable monthly housing payment, and the larger the loan you can secure. However, increasing qualifying income is not just about earning more—it is about presenting your income in the most effective way possible. One of the most powerful ways to scale your borrowing power is by optimizing your deposit flow. This means ensuring that all legitimate income is captured, documented, and presented clearly in your bank statements. Many borrowers unintentionally leave income "on the table" because deposits are not properly structured or documented. For example, payments that are split across multiple accounts, undocumented cash deposits, or transfers that obscure income sources can all reduce the amount of income that lenders are able to use. By consolidating and clarifying your deposit activity, you can increase your qualifying income without changing your actual earnings.

Another key strategy is reducing your expense factor. As discussed in previous chapters, the expense factor determines how much of your gross deposits are considered net income. Lowering this percentage—through documentation such as a CPA-prepared profit and loss statement—can significantly increase your qualifying income. This is one of the most direct ways to scale your borrowing power. Even a small reduction in your expense factor can result in thousands of dollars of additional qualifying income per month.

Debt management also plays a critical role in scaling your loan amount. Your debt-to-income ratio determines how much of your income can be allocated toward your mortgage payment. By reducing or eliminating existing debts, you free up more of your income for housing. For example, paying off a car loan or credit card balance can increase your available monthly capacity, allowing you to qualify for a larger loan. This is often one of the simplest and most effective ways to improve your borrowing power.

Another important factor is reserves. Many lenders require borrowers to have a certain amount of reserves—typically measured in months of mortgage payments—especially for larger loan amounts. Strong reserves not only meet lender requirements but also serve as a compensating factor that can strengthen your application. Demonstrating that you have sufficient funds to cover future payments reduces risk and can support approval for higher loan amounts.

Credit profile is another critical component. While personal bank statement loans are more flexible than traditional loans, your credit score still plays a significant role in determining your loan terms and maximum eligibility. A higher credit score can lead to better interest rates and more favorable guidelines, which in turn can increase your borrowing power. Improving your credit profile before applying can have a meaningful impact on your overall outcome.

Loan structure also matters. Choosing the right loan program, term, and interest rate can influence how much you qualify for. For example, a longer loan term may result in a lower monthly payment, allowing you to qualify for a higher loan amount. Similarly, selecting a program with more flexible debt-to-income limits can increase your borrowing capacity. Understanding these options and working with a knowledgeable loan officer can help you structure your loan in a way that maximizes your potential.

Another advanced strategy is layering multiple strengths. While each individual factor—income, expenses, debt, reserves, credit—contributes to your overall profile, combining them creates a much stronger application. For example, a borrower with strong income, low expenses, minimal debt, and high reserves presents a low-risk profile that lenders are more willing to support with larger loan amounts. The goal is to build a comprehensive financial picture that demonstrates both capacity and stability.

It is also important to think long-term. Scaling your borrowing power is not just about a single transaction—it is about building a foundation for future opportunities. By establishing strong financial habits, maintaining clean bank statements, and documenting your income effectively, you position yourself for ongoing success in the mortgage market. This is especially valuable for borrowers who plan to invest in multiple properties or refinance in the future. Timing can also influence your ability to qualify for larger loan amounts.

Applying when your income is at its peak, your debts are minimized, and your financial profile is strongest can significantly improve your outcome. This requires planning and awareness, but the results can be substantial.

Ultimately, qualifying for larger loan amounts is about strategy. It is about understanding how each component of your financial profile interacts and using that knowledge to your advantage. By applying the principles in this chapter, you can move beyond basic approval and unlock your full borrowing potential.

Real-Life Math Example: Scaling Borrowing Power Step by Step

Let's walk through a detailed real-life example to illustrate how different strategies can increase borrowing power. Imagine a borrower named Michael, who is a self-employed consultant applying for a mortgage using personal bank statements.

Michael's initial financial profile shows total qualifying deposits of $360,000 over 12 months, averaging $30,000 per month. The lender applies a 50 percent expense factor, resulting in a qualifying income of $15,000 per month. Michael has $2,000 in monthly debt obligations, leaving him with $13,000 in available income.

Assuming the lender allows a maximum debt-to-income ratio of 50 percent, Michael can allocate up to $7,500 per month toward his housing payment. Based on current interest rates, this may allow him to qualify for a loan amount of approximately $1,050,000.

Now let's explore how Michael can scale his borrowing power. First, he works with a CPA to document his actual expenses, which are only 30 percent of his income. This reduces his expense factor from 50 percent to 30 percent, increasing his qualifying income from $15,000 to $21,000 per month.

Next, Michael pays off a car loan with a monthly payment of $800, reducing his total monthly debt from $2,000 to $1,200. This increases his available income for housing.

With these changes, his qualifying income is $21,000, and his debts are $1,200, leaving $19,800 in available income. At a 50 percent debt-to-income limit, he can now allocate up to $10,500 per month toward his mortgage.

This increase in allowable payment significantly boosts his borrowing power. Instead of qualifying for a $1,050,000 loan, he may now qualify for a loan amount closer to $1,500,000 or more, depending on other factors.

Now let's take it one step further. Michael improves his credit score, allowing him to secure a slightly lower interest rate. This reduces his monthly payment for a given loan amount, enabling him to qualify for an even larger loan. Additionally, he demonstrates strong reserves, which further strengthens his application and supports approval at the higher level.

Through these combined strategies, Michael increases his borrowing power by nearly $500,000. Importantly, he did not increase his actual income—he optimized how his income was presented, reduced his expenses, and improved his overall financial profile.

This example highlights the power of strategic planning. By understanding how each factor contributes to your loan qualification, you can take deliberate steps to maximize your outcome. Scaling your borrowing power is not about luck—it is about applying the right strategies at the right time.

As you continue through this book, you will gain even deeper insights into how to refine your approach and achieve your financial goals.

Chapter 9

Getting Approved with Credit Challenges Using Personal Bank Statements

One of the most powerful advantages of personal bank statement mortgage loans is their flexibility—not just with income, but also with credit. While traditional mortgage programs often rely heavily on strict credit requirements, personal bank statement loans provide an alternative path for borrowers who may have experienced past credit challenges. This chapter is designed to help you understand how to navigate those challenges, position your financial profile effectively, and still achieve mortgage approval.

Credit challenges can take many forms. Some borrowers may have late payments, high credit utilization, or collections. Others may have experienced more significant events such as bankruptcies, foreclosures, or short sales. In traditional lending, these events can create long waiting periods or even disqualify a borrower entirely. However, in the world of non-QM and bank statement lending, lenders take a more holistic approach. Instead of focusing solely on past credit events, they evaluate the overall risk profile, including income, reserves, and compensating factors.

The first key concept to understand is credit event seasoning. Seasoning refers to the amount of time that has passed since a negative credit event occurred. The more time that has passed, the less impact the event typically has on your loan application. For example, a borrower who had a bankruptcy five years ago but has demonstrated strong financial behavior since then may be viewed much more favorably than someone with a recent event. Lenders want to see that you have recovered and established stability over time.

Another important factor is your current credit behavior. While past events cannot be changed, your recent activity carries significant weight. Consistently making on-time payments, reducing credit card balances, and avoiding new derogatory marks can demonstrate responsibility and improvement. Lenders often focus on the most recent 12 to 24 months of credit history to assess your current financial habits. A strong recent history can offset older negative events and strengthen your application.

Compensating factors play a critical role in overcoming credit challenges. These are strengths in your financial profile that reduce the lender's perceived risk. For example, strong and consistent income demonstrated through bank statements can serve as a powerful compensating factor. High reserves—such as several months of mortgage payments saved in your accounts—can also provide reassurance. A larger down payment can further reduce risk by lowering the loan-to-value ratio. When these factors are combined, they can significantly improve your chances of approval, even with less-than-perfect credit.

Loan structure becomes especially important when dealing with credit challenges. Lenders may adjust certain terms to account for increased risk. This could include requiring a higher down payment, applying a slightly higher interest rate, or limiting the maximum loan-to-value ratio. While these adjustments may not be ideal, they provide a pathway to approval that would not be available through traditional programs. The goal is to get into the market and then improve your position over time, potentially refinancing into better terms later.

Another key strategy is reducing your overall risk profile. This includes paying down existing debts, avoiding new credit inquiries, and maintaining stable financial behavior. Even small improvements can have a meaningful impact. For example, lowering your credit card balances can improve your credit score and reduce your debt-to-income ratio, both of which strengthen your application. These proactive steps demonstrate to lenders that you are managing your finances responsibly. Documentation also plays a role in addressing credit challenges. Providing explanations for past events can help lenders understand the context behind your credit history. For example, if a financial hardship was caused by a temporary situation such as a medical issue or business downturn, explaining how you have recovered can add valuable perspective. The goal is to show that the event was isolated and that you have taken steps to prevent it from happening again.

It is also important to focus on consistency and stability. Lenders want to see that your current financial situation is reliable and sustainable. This includes consistent income, stable account balances, and responsible credit usage. By demonstrating these qualities, you can shift the focus away from past challenges and toward your present strengths.

Another advantage of personal bank statement loans is that they allow lenders to evaluate real cash flow. Even if your credit history is not perfect, strong income and liquidity can provide confidence in your ability to repay the loan. This is one of the key reasons why these programs exist—to provide opportunities for borrowers who are financially capable but do not fit traditional criteria.

As you move forward, it is important to approach the process with a long-term mindset. Getting approved with credit challenges is not just about the immediate transaction—it is about rebuilding and strengthening your financial profile over time. Once you secure a loan, maintaining strong payment history and improving your credit can open the door to better opportunities in the future.

This chapter is about showing you that credit challenges do not define your future. With the right strategies, preparation, and understanding, you can overcome these obstacles and achieve your homeownership goals.

Real-Life Math Example: Qualifying with Credit Challenges and Strong Income

Now, we're going to walk through a detailed real-life example to illustrate how a borrower with credit challenges can still qualify for a mortgage using personal bank statements. Imagine a borrower named Rachel, who is a self-employed hairstylist and salon owner.

Rachel experienced financial difficulties three years ago, resulting in several late payments and a temporary drop in her credit score. However, over the past two years, she has rebuilt her business and established consistent income. She is now applying for a mortgage using 12 months of personal bank statements. Over the 12-month period, Rachel's total qualifying deposits are $240,000, averaging $20,000 per month. The lender applies a 50 percent expense factor, resulting in a qualifying income of $10,000 per month. Rachel has $1,500 in monthly debt obligations, including a car payment and credit card payments.

Using her qualifying income, Rachel's current debt-to-income ratio is 15 percent before adding a mortgage payment. Assuming the lender allows a maximum ratio of 50 percent, she can allocate up to $5,000 per month toward her housing payment.

However, due to her credit challenges, the lender requires a higher down payment and applies a slightly higher interest rate. These adjustments reduce the loan amount she can qualify for compared to a borrower with perfect credit. Based on these factors, Rachel may qualify for a loan amount of approximately $600,000.

Now let's consider how Rachel can improve her situation. First, she pays down her credit card balances, reducing her monthly debt from $1,500 to $1,000. This increases her available income for housing. Next, she provides documentation showing that her business has been stable and growing, strengthening her overall profile.

She also increases her down payment, which reduces the loan-to-value ratio and lowers the lender's risk. With these improvements, the lender may be more comfortable offering slightly better terms, increasing her borrowing power.

In this improved scenario, Rachel's qualifying income remains at $10,000 per month, but her lower debts and stronger profile allow her to allocate more toward her mortgage. She may now qualify for a loan amount closer to $700,000 or more.

This example demonstrates that credit challenges do not eliminate your ability to qualify—they simply require a more strategic approach. By strengthening other areas of your financial profile, you can offset credit concerns and achieve a successful outcome.

As you continue through this book, you will learn how to combine these strategies with everything you have learned so far to create a powerful and well-rounded loan application.

Chapter 10

Advanced Bank Statement Loan Structuring – Engineering Approvals Using Deposits, Expense Ratios, and Investor Guidelines

At this stage in your journey, you are no longer simply learning how to qualify—you are learning how to engineer approvals. Advanced bank statement loan structuring is where strategy, timing, and precision come together. It is the art of taking your existing financial profile and shaping it in a way that aligns perfectly with lender and investor guidelines. This chapter is designed to elevate your understanding from borrower to strategist, giving you the ability to control outcomes rather than react to them.

The foundation of advanced structuring begins with understanding that every lender and investor operates under slightly different guidelines. While the core principles of bank statement lending remain consistent, the interpretation of deposits, expense factors, and qualifying income can vary. Some lenders may be more flexible with expense ratios, while others may be more accommodating with higher debt-to-income limits. The key is not to find a single solution, but to match your financial profile with the lender whose guidelines best support your strengths.

One of the most powerful tools in advanced structuring is deposit engineering. This does not mean manipulating your income—it means organizing and presenting it in the most favorable way possible. For example, consolidating income streams into a primary account can create a clearer deposit pattern. Timing deposits consistently can improve perceived stability. Ensuring that all deposits are properly documented can prevent exclusions. These small adjustments can have a significant impact on how your income is interpreted during underwriting.

Another critical component is strategic expense ratio optimization. As you have learned, the expense factor directly affects your qualifying income. In advanced structuring, you go beyond simply accepting a standard percentage. You actively work to justify a lower ratio through documentation, business positioning, and financial clarity. This may involve working with a CPA, restructuring how expenses are tracked, or demonstrating that your business operates with lower overhead than typical industry standards. The goal is to align your actual financial performance with how it is evaluated by the lender. Debt-to-income ratio management is another area where advanced structuring plays a crucial role. Instead of viewing your existing debts as fixed, you evaluate them strategically. This may involve paying down certain obligations, restructuring payments, or timing your application after reducing key liabilities. Even small changes in your monthly debt can significantly increase your allowable housing payment, which directly impacts your loan amount.

Layering compensating factors is another advanced technique. Lenders evaluate risk holistically, meaning that strengths in one area can offset weaknesses in another. For example, a borrower with slightly higher debt may still qualify if they have strong reserves, excellent credit, and consistent income. By combining multiple strengths—such as clean bank statements, low expense ratios, strong reserves, and stable deposits—you create a profile that is difficult to deny.

Another important concept is scenario planning. Instead of relying on a single approach, advanced borrowers evaluate multiple scenarios to determine the best outcome. For example, you may compare a 12-month analysis versus a 24-month analysis, test different expense ratios, or evaluate how paying off certain debts would impact your qualification. By running these scenarios in advance, you can choose the strategy that produces the highest qualifying income and the most favorable loan terms. Timing becomes even more critical at this level. Advanced structuring often involves preparing your financial profile months in advance of your application. This may include stabilizing deposit patterns, reducing unnecessary transactions, improving credit, and building reserves. By controlling the timing of your application, you ensure that your financial profile is presented at its strongest point.

Investor overlays also play a significant role. These are additional guidelines imposed by lenders or investors beyond standard requirements. Understanding these overlays allows you to avoid potential obstacles and position your file accordingly. For example, some investors may have stricter requirements for large deposits, while others may be more flexible with expense ratios. Knowing these differences allows you to tailor your application to the right lender.

Another advanced strategy is leveraging multiple accounts strategically. While excessive transfers can create confusion, properly structured accounts can enhance clarity. For example, separating income streams into organized channels and then consolidating them into a primary account can create a clean and traceable deposit history. The key is to maintain transparency while reducing complexity.

It is also important to think beyond a single transaction. Advanced structuring is about building a system that supports long-term financial growth. By maintaining clean records, consistent deposits, and strong documentation, you create a foundation that can support future purchases, refinances, and investment opportunities. This long-term perspective allows you to scale your real estate portfolio and financial success over time.

Ultimately, advanced bank statement loan structuring is about control. It is about understanding every variable in the process and using that knowledge to your advantage. When you reach this level, you are no longer limited by standard guidelines—you are working within them strategically to achieve your goals.

This chapter represents the culmination of everything you have learned in this book. It is where knowledge becomes execution, and execution becomes results.

Real-Life Math Example: Engineering a High-Level Loan Approval

Let's walk through a detailed real-life example to illustrate how advanced structuring can transform a borrower's outcome. Imagine a borrower named Anthony, who is a self-employed entrepreneur with multiple income streams.

Anthony's initial financial profile shows total deposits of $600,000 over 12 months, averaging $50,000 per month. At first glance, this appears to position him for a very high loan amount. However, the lender must analyze his deposits and apply standard guidelines.

In the initial scenario, the lender excludes $100,000 in transfers and undocumented deposits, leaving $500,000 in qualifying deposits. This results in an average monthly income of approximately $41,667. Applying a standard 50 percent expense factor reduces his qualifying income to approximately $20,833 per month.

Anthony has $3,000 in monthly debt obligations, leaving $17,833 in available income. At a 50 percent debt-to-income limit, he can allocate approximately $10,417 per month toward his mortgage. This may allow him to qualify for a loan amount of approximately $1.5 million.

Now let's apply advanced structuring strategies. First, Anthony restructures his accounts to eliminate unnecessary transfers and document all income sources. This allows the lender to include an additional $80,000 in deposits, increasing his qualifying deposits to $580,000. His average monthly income rises to approximately $48,333.

Next, Anthony works with a CPA to prepare a profit and loss statement showing that his actual expenses are only 30 percent. This reduces his expense factor from 50 percent to 30 percent, increasing his qualifying income from $20,833 to approximately $33,833 per month. He then pays off a portion of his debt, reducing his monthly obligations from $3,000 to $1,500. This increases his available income for housing.

With these changes, Anthony's qualifying income is $33,833, and his debts are $1,500, leaving $32,333 in available income. At a 50 percent debt-to-income limit, he can now allocate approximately $16,917 per month toward his mortgage.

This increased payment capacity significantly boosts his borrowing power. Instead of qualifying for a $1.5 million loan, he may now qualify for a loan amount exceeding $2.5 million, depending on interest rates and other factors.

Additionally, Anthony demonstrates strong reserves and a solid credit profile, further strengthening his application. These compensating factors may allow him to secure better terms and increase his approval confidence.

This example illustrates the power of advanced structuring. By optimizing deposits, reducing expense ratios, managing debt, and aligning with lender guidelines, Anthony increases his borrowing power by over $1 million—all without increasing his actual income.

This is the level of control and strategy that defines advanced bank statement lending. It is not about working harder—it is about working smarter and understanding how to position your financial profile for maximum success.

As you complete this book, you now have the knowledge and tools to approach personal bank statement mortgage loans at the highest level. The next step is to apply these strategies and take action toward your financial goals.

Chapter 11

Pre-Approval, Underwriting, and Closing – Navigating the Bank Statement Loan Process Step by Step

Understanding how to qualify using personal bank statements is only part of the journey. The other critical piece is knowing how to successfully move through the mortgage process from pre-approval to closing. Many borrowers underestimate how important this phase is, but in reality, this is where approvals are won or lost. Even a strong financial profile can face delays or complications if the process is not handled strategically. This chapter will guide you step by step through the entire process so you can navigate it with confidence and control.

The journey begins with pre-approval. This is the stage where your financial profile is evaluated to determine how much you may qualify for. In a personal bank statement loan, pre-approval involves reviewing your bank statements, estimating your qualifying income, and identifying any potential issues early. This is not just a formality—it is a strategic opportunity. A strong pre-approval allows you to understand your price range, strengthen your position as a buyer, and move quickly when you find the right property.

During pre-approval, your loan officer will analyze your deposits, apply an estimated expense factor, and calculate your preliminary qualifying income. They will also review your credit, debts, and reserves to determine your overall profile. This is the stage where you can test different scenarios, such as using 12 months versus 24 months of bank statements or providing additional documentation to reduce your expense factor. The goal is to identify the strongest possible structure before moving forward.

Once you have a pre-approval, the next step is submitting your full loan application. This is where your documentation becomes critical. You will provide your bank statements, identification, credit authorization, and any supporting documents such as profit and loss statements, letters of explanation, and business documentation. The completeness and organization of your file at this stage can significantly impact how smoothly the process moves forward.

After submission, your file enters underwriting. This is the most detailed and important phase of the process. The underwriter is responsible for verifying your information, analyzing your bank statements, and ensuring that your loan meets all guidelines. They will review your deposits, confirm your qualifying income, evaluate your debt-to-income ratio, and assess your overall risk profile. Underwriting is where many borrowers experience delays, often due to missing or unclear documentation. This is why preparation is so important. If your bank statements include large deposits, irregular patterns, or potential red flags, the underwriter will request explanations and supporting documents. These requests are known as conditions. The faster and more clearly you respond to these conditions, the smoother the process will be.

One of the key strategies during underwriting is responsiveness. Delays often occur when borrowers take too long to provide requested documents or provide incomplete information. By staying organized and responding quickly, you can keep your loan moving forward. Think of underwriting as a collaborative process—you are working with the lender to demonstrate that your loan meets all requirements.

Another important aspect of underwriting is consistency. All of your documents must align and tell the same story. If your bank statements, profit and loss statement, and explanations are consistent, the underwriter can move forward with confidence. If there are discrepancies, additional questions will arise. Ensuring that your documentation is accurate and consistent before submission can prevent many of these issues.

Once your conditions are satisfied, your loan moves to approval. At this stage, the underwriter has determined that your loan meets all guidelines, and you are cleared to move forward. However, there may still be final conditions to complete, such as verifying employment, confirming assets, or updating documents. This is often referred to as "clear to close."

The closing phase is where everything comes together. Your loan documents are prepared, and you will review and sign them. This includes your loan agreement, disclosures, and other required documents. Once everything is signed and finalized, the loan is funded, and the transaction is complete. This is the moment where your preparation, strategy, and effort result in a successful outcome.

It is important to understand that each stage of the process builds on the previous one. A strong pre-approval leads to a smoother underwriting process, which leads to a faster closing. By approaching each step with preparation and strategy, you can minimize stress and maximize efficiency.

Another key concept is control. While the mortgage process involves multiple parties—loan officers, underwriters, processors, and closing agents—you still have a significant level of control over the outcome. By providing clear documentation, responding quickly, and maintaining consistency, you influence how your file is perceived and processed.

Communication is also critical. Staying in regular contact with your loan officer and understanding what is required at each stage can help you avoid surprises. Asking questions, clarifying expectations, and staying informed allows you to move through the process with confidence.

Ultimately, the mortgage process is not just about meeting requirements—it is about presenting your financial story in a way that meets those requirements clearly and convincingly. When you understand the process and take an active role in it, you position yourself for success.

This chapter is your roadmap from pre-approval to closing. By following these steps and applying the strategies you have learned, you can navigate the process smoothly and achieve your goal of homeownership or investment.

Real-Life Math Example: From Pre-Approval to Closing with Strategic Adjustments

Now, we're going to walk through a detailed real-life example to illustrate how a borrower moves through the mortgage process and how strategic decisions impact the final outcome.

Imagine a borrower named Carlos, who is self-employed and applying for a mortgage using personal bank statements.

During the pre-approval stage, Carlos provides 12 months of bank statements showing total deposits of $300,000, averaging $25,000 per month. The loan officer applies a 50 percent expense factor, resulting in a qualifying income of $12,500 per month. Carlos has $2,000 in monthly debt obligations, leaving $10,500 available for housing.

Based on this initial analysis, Carlos is pre-approved for a loan amount of approximately $800,000. This gives him a clear understanding of his budget and allows him to begin searching for a property.

As Carlos moves into the application stage, he provides additional documentation, including a CPA-prepared profit and loss statement showing that his actual expenses are only 35 percent. This allows the lender to adjust his expense factor from 50 percent to 35 percent.

Underwriting begins, and the underwriter reviews his bank statements in detail. They identify $40,000 in deposits that require clarification. Carlos provides invoices and contracts to support these deposits, allowing them to be included in his qualifying income. This increases his total qualifying deposits to $340,000, or approximately $28,333 per month.

Applying the 35 percent expense factor results in a qualifying income of approximately $18,417 per month. With $2,000 in debts, Carlos now has $16,417 available for housing. At a 50 percent debt-to-income limit, he can allocate approximately $9,200 per month toward his mortgage. This increased capacity allows Carlos to qualify for a loan amount closer to $1,200,000, significantly higher than his initial pre-approval. This demonstrates how additional documentation and strategic adjustments during underwriting can improve outcomes.

Carlos responds quickly to all underwriting conditions, providing clear and consistent documentation. This allows his loan to move smoothly through the process. Once all conditions are satisfied, he receives final approval and proceeds to closing.

At closing, Carlos signs his loan documents, and the loan is funded. He successfully purchases his property with a loan amount that reflects his true earning potential, not just the initial estimate.

This example highlights the dynamic nature of the mortgage process. Your initial pre-approval is not necessarily your final outcome. By actively participating in the process, providing documentation, and making strategic adjustments, you can improve your results and maximize your borrowing power.

As you complete this chapter, you now understand not only how to qualify, but how to successfully navigate the entire process from start to finish.

Chapter 12

Long-Term Strategy – Using Personal Bank Statement Loans to Build Wealth and Financial Freedom

By the time you reach this chapter, you have developed a deep understanding of how personal bank statement mortgage loans work, how to qualify, and how to strategically structure your financial profile. Now it is time to take the next step—thinking beyond a single loan and focusing on long-term wealth creation. Personal bank statement loans are not just a solution for getting approved; they are a powerful tool that can be used repeatedly to build a real estate portfolio, increase financial leverage, and create lasting financial independence.

One of the most important mindset shifts at this stage is moving from a transactional approach to a strategic approach. Many borrowers focus on getting approved for one property, whether it is a primary residence or an investment property. While that is a great starting point, the true power of these loans comes from their ability to be used over and over again as your income grows and your financial profile strengthens. Each successful transaction becomes a stepping stone toward greater opportunities. The foundation of long-term strategy is consistency. The same principles that helped you qualify for your first loan—clean bank statements, consistent deposits, optimized expense factors, and strong documentation—will continue to support your future transactions. By maintaining these habits, you create a financial profile that is always ready for the next opportunity. This allows you to move quickly when new deals arise and positions you as a strong borrower in the eyes of lenders.

Another key component of long-term strategy is reinvestment. Instead of viewing your income as something to spend, you begin to view it as a resource to deploy strategically. For example, the income generated from your business can be used to acquire real estate assets that produce additional income. Over time, these assets can create a compounding effect, where each property contributes to your overall financial growth. Personal bank statement loans make this possible by allowing you to qualify based on your real income, even if it is not fully reflected in your tax returns.

Scaling your portfolio requires planning and discipline. Each new property adds both opportunity and responsibility. Lenders will evaluate your entire financial picture, including your existing loans, rental income, and reserves. By managing your portfolio carefully—ensuring that each property is financially sustainable—you can continue to qualify for additional loans. This means choosing properties that generate positive cash flow, maintaining adequate reserves, and avoiding overextension.

Refinancing is another powerful tool in your long-term strategy. As your properties increase in value and your equity grows, you may have the opportunity to refinance and access that equity. This can provide capital for additional investments, debt consolidation, or other financial goals. Personal bank statement loans can also be used for refinancing, allowing you to leverage your income and assets in a flexible way.

Another important concept is diversification. While real estate can be a powerful wealth-building tool, it is important to consider how it fits into your overall financial strategy. Diversifying your investments across different property types, locations, and income streams can reduce risk and increase stability. Personal bank statement loans provide the flexibility to explore a variety of opportunities, from primary residences to investment properties and beyond.

Timing continues to play a critical role. Just as you learned to time your application for maximum qualifying income, you can also time your investments to align with market conditions and your financial readiness. This includes monitoring interest rates, property values, and your own financial performance. By staying informed and prepared, you can take advantage of opportunities as they arise.

Another key element of long-term success is building relationships. Working with experienced loan officers, real estate agents, and financial professionals can provide valuable insights and support. These relationships can help you identify opportunities, navigate challenges, and make informed decisions. Over time, your network becomes an important asset in your overall strategy.

It is also important to maintain a focus on risk management. While leverage can amplify your returns, it also increases your exposure. Ensuring that you have sufficient reserves, maintaining stable income, and avoiding excessive debt are essential components of a sustainable strategy. The goal is not just to grow quickly, but to grow responsibly.

As your portfolio expands, your financial profile becomes more complex. This is where advanced structuring and documentation strategies continue to play a role. By maintaining clear and organized records, you can navigate this complexity and continue to qualify for new opportunities. The principles you have learned throughout this book remain relevant at every stage of your journey. Ultimately, personal bank statement mortgage loans are a gateway to a broader financial strategy. They allow you to leverage your income, access opportunities, and build wealth in a way that aligns with your unique financial situation. By thinking long-term and applying these strategies consistently, you can create a path toward financial freedom.

This chapter is about vision. It is about seeing beyond the immediate transaction and understanding how each step contributes to a larger goal. With the knowledge and tools you now have, you are equipped to take that next step and build a future defined by opportunity and growth.

Real-Life Math Example: Building a Real Estate Portfolio Using Bank Statement Loans

Let's walk through a detailed real-life example to illustrate how personal bank statement loans can be used to build long-term wealth. Imagine a borrower named Jonathan, who is a self-employed business owner with consistent income.

Jonathan's initial financial profile shows total deposits of $480,000 over 12 months, averaging $40,000 per month. After applying a 40 percent expense factor, his qualifying income is $24,000 per month. He has minimal debt, allowing him to allocate a significant portion of his income toward housing.

In his first transaction, Jonathan uses this income to qualify for a loan amount of approximately $1,200,000 to purchase a primary residence. He makes a 20 percent down payment, securing the property and establishing his first major asset.

Over the next year, Jonathan continues to generate strong income and maintains clean bank statements. He also builds equity in his home as property values increase. After 12 months, he applies for a second loan to purchase an investment property. Using updated bank statements showing similar or increased income, he qualifies for an additional loan of $800,000.

The investment property generates rental income, which helps offset the mortgage payment and contributes to his overall financial stability. Jonathan now has two properties, both of which are supported by his income and structured strategically.

After another year, Jonathan explores refinancing his primary residence. Due to increased property value, he is able to access $200,000 in equity through a cash-out refinance. He uses these funds as a down payment for a third property, further expanding his portfolio.

At this stage, Jonathan's financial profile includes multiple income streams—his business income and rental income from his properties. His total monthly income has increased, and he continues to qualify for additional opportunities. By maintaining strong documentation and financial discipline, he is able to leverage personal bank statement loans to scale his portfolio.

Over time, the combined value of his properties increases, and his equity grows. The rental income from his investment properties provides additional cash flow, reducing his reliance on his primary business income. This creates a more diversified and resilient financial position.

This example demonstrates how personal bank statement loans can be used not just for a single transaction, but as part of a long-term wealth-building strategy. By reinvesting income, leveraging equity, and maintaining strong financial habits, borrowers can create a compounding effect that leads to significant financial growth.

As you complete this book, you now have the knowledge, strategies, and vision to apply these principles in your own life. The next step is to take action and begin building your path toward financial freedom.

Chapter 13

Common Mistakes to Avoid and How to Protect Your Loan Approval

As you reach this stage in your journey, you have gained the knowledge and strategies needed to qualify for a personal bank statement mortgage loan and even scale your borrowing power. However, one of the most important factors in achieving success is avoiding the common mistakes that can delay, weaken, or completely derail your approval. Many borrowers do not fail because they lack income or opportunity—they fail because of avoidable errors in preparation, timing, or financial behavior. This chapter is designed to help you identify those mistakes and protect your loan from unnecessary risk.

One of the most common mistakes is waiting too long to prepare. Many borrowers begin organizing their finances only after they decide to apply for a loan. By that point, their bank statements already reflect months of unstructured activity, making it difficult to correct issues retroactively. The reality is that personal bank statement loans require forward planning. Your financial profile is built over time, not in a few weeks. By preparing months in advance—cleaning up deposits, reducing unnecessary transfers, and documenting income—you can present a much stronger application. Another major mistake is assuming that all deposits will count as income. As you have learned, lenders carefully analyze deposits and exclude those that cannot be verified or are not consistent with income. Borrowers who rely on total deposit amounts without understanding this process often overestimate their qualifying income. This can lead to unrealistic expectations and disappointment during underwriting. The key is to understand how deposits are evaluated and to ensure that your income is clearly documented and structured.

Commingling funds without awareness is another frequent issue. While mixing business and personal transactions is common, excessive commingling can create confusion and reduce qualifying income. For example, frequent transfers between accounts or deposits that are not clearly tied to income can lead to exclusions. This does not mean you must completely separate your accounts, but it does mean you should be intentional about how your income flows and how it is presented.

Large, unexplained deposits are another critical mistake. These deposits often trigger underwriting conditions and may be excluded if they cannot be documented. Borrowers sometimes assume that a large deposit will strengthen their application, but without proper documentation, it can have the opposite effect. The solution is simple: ensure that every significant deposit can be explained and supported with documentation such as invoices, contracts, or payment records.

Another common mistake is neglecting expense factor optimization. Many borrowers accept the default expense ratio without realizing that it can be adjusted. This can significantly reduce their qualifying income. By providing a CPA-prepared profit and loss statement or other supporting documentation, borrowers can often reduce their expense factor and increase their income. Failing to take advantage of this opportunity can result in a lower loan amount than what is actually possible.

Debt mismanagement is another area where borrowers often lose potential. Carrying unnecessary debt increases your debt-to-income ratio and reduces your borrowing capacity. Some borrowers overlook the impact of small monthly payments, not realizing that even a few hundred dollars can affect their loan amount. By strategically paying down or eliminating certain debts before applying, you can improve your financial profile and increase your approval potential.

Timing mistakes can also have a significant impact. Applying for a loan during a period of inconsistent income, high expenses, or recent financial changes can weaken your application. For example, if your income has recently increased, it may be beneficial to wait until your bank statements reflect that growth. Conversely, if you anticipate a temporary decline, applying sooner may be the better option. Understanding and controlling timing is a key part of a successful strategy.

Another critical mistake is failing to respond quickly and clearly during underwriting. Delays in providing requested documents or incomplete responses can slow down the process and create additional scrutiny. Underwriting is a time-sensitive phase, and responsiveness is essential. By staying organized and prepared, you can move through this stage efficiently and maintain momentum toward closing.

Overconfidence can also be a hidden risk. Some borrowers assume that strong income alone guarantees approval, but lenders evaluate multiple factors, including credit, reserves, and overall risk. Ignoring these elements can lead to unexpected challenges. A well-rounded approach that addresses all aspects of your financial profile is essential.

Another mistake is focusing only on approval and not on sustainability. Qualifying for a loan is important, but ensuring that you can comfortably manage the payments is equally critical. Overextending yourself financially can create long-term challenges. The goal is not just to get approved—it is to build a stable and sustainable financial future. Finally, one of the most important mistakes to avoid is failing to think long-term. Each loan you secure becomes part of your financial history and affects your future opportunities. By making strategic decisions, maintaining clean financial records, and managing your obligations responsibly, you create a foundation for ongoing success.

This chapter is about awareness and protection. By understanding these common mistakes and taking steps to avoid them, you can safeguard your loan approval and position yourself for success.

Real-Life Math Example: How Mistakes Reduce Loan Approval and How to Correct Them

Now, we're going to walk through a detailed real-life example to illustrate how common mistakes can impact a borrower's outcome and how correcting them can lead to significant improvement. Imagine a borrower named Steven, who is a self-employed photographer applying for a mortgage using personal bank statements.

Steven's initial financial profile shows total deposits of $300,000 over 12 months, averaging $25,000 per month. However, his bank statements include several issues. First,

$70,000 of his deposits are transfers between accounts, which are excluded. This reduces his qualifying deposits to $230,000. Next, he has $30,000 in large, unexplained deposits that cannot be documented, which are also excluded. This brings his qualifying deposits down to $200,000.

Dividing $200,000 by 12 months results in an average monthly income of approximately $16,667. The lender applies a 50 percent expense factor, reducing his qualifying income to approximately $8,333 per month. Steven also has $2,500 in monthly debt obligations, leaving $5,833 available for housing.

Based on this profile, Steven may qualify for a loan amount of approximately $500,000 to $550,000. While this is a viable approval, it is far below what his total deposits initially suggested.

Now let's see how correcting these mistakes changes the outcome. Steven begins by restructuring his accounts to eliminate unnecessary transfers. This allows the lender to include an additional $60,000 in deposits, increasing his qualifying deposits to $260,000. He also gathers documentation for the previously unexplained deposits, allowing $20,000 of that amount to be included. His total qualifying deposits now increase to $280,000.

This results in an average monthly income of approximately $23,333. Next, Steven works with a CPA to prepare a profit and loss statement showing that his actual expenses are 35 percent. This reduces his expense factor from 50 percent to 35 percent, increasing his qualifying income to approximately $15,167 per month.

He then pays off a credit card and reduces his monthly debt from $2,500 to $1,500. This increases his available income for housing to approximately $13,667. At a 50 percent debt-to-income limit, he can now allocate approximately $7,583 per month toward his mortgage.

With these improvements, Steven's borrowing power increases significantly. Instead of qualifying for a $500,000 loan, he may now qualify for a loan amount closer to $900,000 or more, depending on other factors. This represents an increase of over $350,000 in borrowing capacity.

This example clearly demonstrates how common mistakes can reduce qualifying income and how correcting them can dramatically improve outcomes. By understanding and avoiding these pitfalls, you can protect your loan approval and maximize your financial potential.

As you complete this chapter, you now have the awareness needed to navigate the process with confidence and precision.

Chapter 14

Creating a Repeatable System – Turning Bank Statement Loans into a Scalable Financial Machine

By now, you understand how to qualify, structure, and optimize a personal bank statement mortgage loan. But the highest level of success comes when you stop treating this process as a one-time event and begin turning it into a repeatable system. This chapter is about building that system—one that allows you to consistently qualify, close, and scale over time without starting from scratch each time you pursue a new opportunity.

A repeatable system begins with standardization. Instead of approaching each loan as a new and unpredictable process, you create a consistent framework for how your finances are managed and presented. This includes maintaining clean bank statements, consistent deposit patterns, organized documentation, and a clear understanding of your expense ratios. When these elements are standardized, each future loan becomes easier, faster, and more predictable.

The first step in building this system is establishing a primary income flow structure. This means creating a clear path for how your income is received, deposited, and recorded. Ideally, all income flows into one primary account in a consistent and organized manner. This creates a clean deposit history that lenders can easily analyze. By maintaining this structure over time, you eliminate confusion and maximize the amount of income that can be used for qualification.

The second component is documentation automation. Instead of scrambling to gather documents each time you apply for a loan, you create a system for continuously tracking and organizing your financial records. This includes maintaining updated profit and loss statements, saving invoices and contracts, and documenting large or irregular deposits as they occur. By doing this consistently, you ensure that your file is always ready for review.

Another key element is expense optimization as an ongoing practice. Rather than addressing your expense factor only when applying for a loan, you continuously monitor and manage your business expenses. This allows you to maintain a lower expense ratio over time, which directly increases your qualifying income. Working with a CPA on a regular basis can help you track and document your expenses accurately, ensuring that your financial profile reflects your true earning potential.

Debt management should also be part of your system. Instead of reacting to your debt situation when applying for a loan, you proactively manage your liabilities. This includes paying down high-impact debts, avoiding unnecessary new obligations, and maintaining a debt profile that supports your borrowing goals. By keeping your debt-to-income ratio optimized, you position yourself to qualify for larger loan amounts consistently.

Another critical component is reserve building. Lenders often require reserves, especially for larger or multiple properties. By making reserve accumulation part of your ongoing financial strategy, you ensure that you are always prepared for new opportunities. This also strengthens your overall financial profile and provides a safety net that supports long-term stability.

Timing and sequencing become even more important in a repeatable system. Instead of applying for loans randomly, you plan your transactions strategically. This may involve spacing out purchases, aligning applications with periods of strong income, and preparing your financial profile in advance. By controlling the timing of your applications, you maximize your chances of approval and optimize your results.

Another advanced element is portfolio awareness. As you acquire more properties, your overall financial picture becomes more complex. Each loan affects your future borrowing capacity. By tracking your portfolio, understanding your obligations, and planning your next steps accordingly, you can continue to scale without overextending yourself. This requires a balance between growth and sustainability.

Relationships also play a key role in a repeatable system. Working with the same loan officers, lenders, and financial professionals over time can create efficiencies and improve outcomes. These professionals become familiar with your financial profile and can help you navigate each transaction more effectively. Building a strong team around you is an important part of long-term success.

Another important concept is continuous improvement. After each loan, you should evaluate what worked well and what could be improved. This might include refining your documentation process, improving your deposit structure, or adjusting your timing. By learning from each experience, you strengthen your system and increase your efficiency over time.

Technology can also support your system. Using tools to track income, manage expenses, and organize documents can streamline your process and reduce errors. The more organized and efficient your system is, the easier it becomes to scale.

Ultimately, a repeatable system transforms the way you approach personal bank statement loans. Instead of reacting to each opportunity, you are prepared for it. Instead of solving problems during underwriting, you prevent them in advance. This level of preparation allows you to move quickly, confidently, and consistently toward your financial goals.

This chapter is about mastery. It is about taking everything you have learned and turning it into a system that works for you—not just once, but repeatedly over time.

Real-Life Math Example: Building a Repeatable Loan System Over Multiple Transactions

Let's walk through a detailed real-life example to illustrate how a repeatable system can create long-term financial growth. Imagine a borrower named Olivia, who is a self-employed consultant with consistent income.

In her first year, Olivia's total deposits are $360,000, averaging $30,000 per month. With a 40 percent expense factor, her qualifying income is $18,000 per month. She has minimal debt, allowing her to qualify for a loan amount of approximately $900,000. She uses this to purchase her first property.

Instead of stopping there, Olivia begins implementing a repeatable system. She consolidates her income into a single account, maintains clean deposit patterns, and works with a CPA to document her expenses accurately. She also begins saving a portion of her income to build reserves. In the following year, her income remains consistent at $30,000 per month, but her documentation improves. Her CPA-prepared profit and loss statement shows that her expenses are only 30 percent. This increases her qualifying income to $21,000 per month.

At the same time, Olivia pays down a small amount of debt and increases her reserves. With these improvements, she qualifies for a second loan of approximately $1,100,000. She uses this to purchase an investment property.

Now Olivia has two properties and a stronger financial profile. She continues to follow her system—maintaining clean accounts, documenting income, and managing expenses. Over time, her income grows to $40,000 per month, and her expense ratio remains at 30 percent. This results in a qualifying income of $28,000 per month.

With this higher income and strong reserves, Olivia qualifies for a third loan of approximately $1,500,000. She adds another property to her portfolio, further increasing her assets and income potential.

Over a period of several years, Olivia's consistent application of her system allows her to acquire multiple properties and build significant equity. Her portfolio generates additional income, which further strengthens her financial position and supports future growth. This example demonstrates how a repeatable system can transform a single loan into a scalable financial strategy. By maintaining consistency, optimizing her financial profile, and planning strategically, Olivia is able to grow her borrowing power and achieve long-term success.

As you complete this chapter, you now have the blueprint for turning personal bank statement loans into a repeatable and scalable system. The next step is to apply this system and continue building your financial future.

Chapter 15

Final Strategy – From Loan Approval to Financial Independence Using Bank Statement Loans

You have now reached the final chapter of this book, and with it, the culmination of everything you have learned. From understanding deposit analysis and expense factors to structuring your accounts, avoiding red flags, navigating underwriting, and building a repeatable system, you now possess a complete framework for using personal bank statement mortgage loans at a high level. This final chapter is about bringing all of those pieces together into one clear, powerful strategy—one that moves beyond approval and into true financial independence.

The first principle of this final strategy is clarity of purpose. Getting approved for a loan is not the end goal—it is the beginning. The real objective is to use that approval as a tool to create income, build equity, and establish long-term financial stability. Whether your focus is on owning your primary residence, building a rental portfolio, or creating multiple income streams, your loan becomes a stepping stone toward something greater. When you approach the process with this mindset, every decision becomes more intentional and aligned with your long-term goals.

The second principle is control. Throughout this book, you have learned that your financial profile is not fixed—it is something you can shape. You control how your income is deposited, how your expenses are documented, how your accounts are structured, and how your application is presented. This level of control allows you to influence your qualifying income, your loan terms, and your overall outcome. The more you exercise this control, the more predictable and successful your results become.

The third principle is leverage. Personal bank statement loans allow you to leverage your income in a way that traditional loans often cannot. Instead of being limited by what is shown on your tax returns, you can qualify based on your actual cash flow. This opens the door to opportunities that would otherwise be out of reach. When used strategically, leverage allows you to acquire assets that generate income and appreciate over time, creating a compounding effect that accelerates your financial growth.

Another key component of this strategy is momentum. Each successful transaction builds on the last. Your first loan leads to your first property. That property builds equity and, potentially, income. That income and equity support your next loan, and the cycle continues. Momentum is created through consistency—consistent income, consistent financial management, and consistent application of the strategies you have learned. Over time, this momentum becomes a powerful force that drives your financial progress.

Risk management remains an essential part of the equation. While leverage and growth are important, they must be balanced with stability and sustainability. This means maintaining adequate reserves, ensuring that your properties are financially viable, and avoiding overextension. Financial independence is not just about growth—it is about maintaining control and resilience in the face of changing conditions.

Another important element is adaptability. The mortgage market, interest rates, and lending guidelines will continue to evolve. Your ability to adapt to these changes will determine your long-term success. By staying informed, maintaining strong financial habits, and working with knowledgeable professionals, you can navigate these changes and continue to find opportunities.

Your network also becomes increasingly valuable as you progress. Relationships with loan officers, real estate agents, CPAs, and other professionals can provide insights, opportunities, and support. These relationships can help you identify deals, optimize your financial strategy, and navigate complex situations. Building and maintaining this network is an important part of your long-term success.

Another critical factor is discipline. The strategies outlined in this book are powerful, but they require consistent application. This means maintaining clean bank statements, documenting your income, managing your expenses, and planning your transactions strategically. Discipline ensures that your system continues to work effectively over time.

Vision ties everything together. Financial independence is not achieved through a single action—it is the result of a series of intentional decisions made over time. By maintaining a clear vision of your goals and aligning your actions with that vision, you create a path that leads to long-term success. Each loan, each property, and each financial decision becomes part of a larger strategy.

As you move forward, remember that you are not starting from zero. You now have a complete understanding of how to navigate personal bank statement mortgage loans at every level. You have the tools to qualify, optimize, and scale. The next step is to apply these tools consistently and strategically.

This chapter is not just a conclusion—it is a beginning. It marks the transition from learning to execution, from understanding to action. With the knowledge you have gained, you are equipped to take control of your financial future and build a path toward independence.

Real-Life Math Example: From First Loan to Financial Independence

Now, we're going to walk through a comprehensive real-life example that brings together everything you have learned in this book. Imagine a borrower named Marcus, who is a self-employed entrepreneur with consistent income.

In the beginning, Marcus has total deposits of $360,000 over 12 months, averaging $30,000 per month. With a 40 percent expense factor, his qualifying income is $18,000 per month. He has $2,000 in monthly debt, leaving $16,000 available for housing. Based on this, he qualifies for a loan amount of approximately $1,000,000 and purchases his first property.

Marcus continues to apply the strategies from this book. He maintains clean bank statements, documents his income, and works with a CPA to reduce his expense factor to 30 percent. His income grows to $40,000 per month, and his qualifying income increases to $28,000 per month.

With this improved profile, Marcus qualifies for a second loan of approximately $1,500,000 and purchases an investment property. This property generates rental income, which helps offset his expenses and contributes to his overall financial stability.

Over time, Marcus builds equity in both properties. He refinances one of them, accessing $300,000 in equity, which he uses as a down payment for a third property. His portfolio continues to grow, and his income becomes more diversified.

As Marcus acquires more properties, his rental income increases, reducing his reliance on his primary business. His total monthly income—including business and rental income—reaches $50,000. With a well-structured financial profile and strong reserves, he continues to qualify for additional opportunities.

After several years, Marcus owns multiple properties with significant equity and generates substantial passive income. His financial position is stable, diversified, and scalable. He has moved beyond relying solely on active income and has created a system that supports long-term financial independence.

This example illustrates the power of applying these strategies consistently over time. Each step builds on the last, creating a compounding effect that accelerates growth. By leveraging personal bank statement loans, optimizing financial structure, and maintaining discipline, borrowers can transform their financial trajectory. As you complete this book, you now have a complete roadmap—from understanding the fundamentals to executing an advanced, long-term strategy. The next step is to take action and begin building your own path toward financial independence.

Final Thoughts

As you reach the end of this journey, it is important to pause and recognize what you have accomplished. You have not simply read a book—you have built a new level of understanding about how income, lending, and financial strategy truly work in the modern world. You now see beyond traditional limitations. You understand that qualifying for a mortgage is not just about fitting into a rigid system, but about learning how to position yourself within a flexible one. This shift in perspective alone has the power to change your financial future.

Throughout this series, you have learned that your bank statements are more than just records—they are a reflection of your financial story. Every deposit, every pattern, every decision you make with your money contributes to how that story is told. And more importantly, you now understand that you have control over that narrative. You are no longer at the mercy of outdated systems that fail to capture the reality of modern income. Instead, you have the knowledge to present your financial profile in a way that reflects your true earning power.

You have also learned that approval is not an accident. It is the result of preparation, strategy, and consistency. From structuring your accounts to optimizing your expense factor, from documenting your income to avoiding red flags, every step you take contributes to your overall outcome. When you approach the process intentionally, you eliminate uncertainty and replace it with clarity. You move from hoping for approval to expecting it, because you understand exactly what is required and how to deliver it.

But perhaps the most important lesson in this entire journey is that this is not just about getting a loan. It is about what that loan represents. It represents access. It represents opportunity. It represents the ability to leverage your income to create something greater. Whether that means owning your home, building a portfolio of investment properties, or creating multiple streams of income, the loan is simply the tool. The real power lies in how you use it.

Financial growth is rarely the result of a single decision. It is the result of a series of consistent, intentional actions over time. Each step you take builds on the last. Each improvement you make strengthens your position. Each opportunity you seize moves you closer to your goals. This is how momentum is created. And once that momentum begins, it becomes one of your greatest assets.

You have also seen that success in this space is not reserved for a select few. It is available to anyone who is willing to learn, prepare, and apply the right strategies. You do not need perfect circumstances. You do not need traditional income. What you need is clarity, discipline, and the willingness to take control of your financial future. These are qualities that you can develop and strengthen over time.

As you move forward, it is important to stay focused on sustainability. Growth is powerful, but it must be balanced with stability. Building wealth is not just about acquiring assets—it is about maintaining them, managing them, and ensuring that they support your long-term goals. This means making thoughtful decisions, maintaining reserves, and avoiding unnecessary risk. True financial independence is built on a foundation that is both strong and flexible.

Another key takeaway is the importance of adaptability. The financial world will continue to change. Lending guidelines will evolve, markets will shift, and new opportunities will emerge. The knowledge you have gained in this book gives you a framework that can adapt to those changes. By staying informed and continuing to refine your strategy, you can navigate any environment with confidence.

Your journey does not end here—it evolves. The principles you have learned are not one-time actions; they are ongoing practices. Maintaining clean financial records, documenting your income, managing your expenses, and planning your next move are habits that will continue to serve you. Over time, these habits become second nature, and your financial system becomes more efficient and effective.

It is also important to recognize the value of patience. While some results may come quickly, true financial transformation takes time. Each step forward, no matter how small, contributes to your overall progress. By staying consistent and committed, you allow the compounding effect of your efforts to work in your favor. This is where long-term success is built.

At the same time, do not underestimate the importance of taking action. Knowledge without action has no impact. The strategies you have learned only become powerful when they are applied. Whether your next step is organizing your bank statements, speaking with a loan officer, or planning your first property purchase, the key is to begin. Progress is created through movement.

You are now in a position where you can approach your financial future with confidence and clarity. You understand the process. You understand the strategy. And most importantly, you understand your role in making it happen. This level of awareness is what separates those who struggle from those who succeed. As you continue on this path, remember that every decision you make has the potential to move you forward. Each improvement, each adjustment, each opportunity builds on the last. Over time, these decisions create a trajectory that leads to greater freedom, greater stability, and greater control over your life.

This is the true value of what you have learned. It is not just about mortgages or bank statements. It is about understanding how to use your resources, your knowledge, and your opportunities to create a life that aligns with your goals. It is about turning information into action, and action into results.

The path to financial independence is not a straight line, but it is a path that you now know how to navigate. You have the tools, the strategies, and the mindset to move forward with purpose. The next chapter of your journey is yours to create.

Take what you have learned, apply it with intention, and continue building.

How to Get a Personalized Bank Statement Mortgage Review

If you found this book helpful, you may want to see how these strategies apply to your specific financial situation.

Bank statement mortgage lending is highly customized—your deposits, income patterns, expense ratios, credit profile, property type, and long-term goals all play a role in determining what you qualify for and how your loan should be structured.

Every borrower's situation is different. The way your income flows through your accounts, how your business operates, your credit history, the property you are purchasing or refinancing, and current lender guidelines all impact your options. The strategies and examples in this book are designed to teach you how bank statement mortgage loans work—but your actual qualifying income, loan amount, and loan structure can only be determined by analyzing your real financial profile.

If you would like a no-obligation Bank Statement Mortgage review, you can request one here:

Email: info@FinibiMortgage.com

A licensed mortgage broker will review your bank statements, income structure, credit profile, and goals, and explain what bank statement mortgage options may be available to you—including:

• 12-month and 24-month bank statement programs• Personal vs business bank statement qualification• Primary residence and investment property financing• Cash-out refinance and equity access strategies• Advanced structuring to maximize qualifying income

No cost. No pressure. No obligation.

Sincerely,

Joseph G. Correa

Finibi Mortgage Inc.

Licensed Mortgage Broker

About the Author

Joseph G. Correa is a licensed mortgage broker and the founder of Finibi Mortgage, a Florida-based brokerage specializing in bank statement mortgage loans, non-QM lending, and strategic real estate financing solutions for self-employed borrowers, entrepreneurs, and investors.

With more than two decades of experience in mortgage lending, underwriting, and deal structuring, Joseph has helped thousands of clients qualify for real estate using alternative income documentation, unlocking opportunities that traditional lending often restricts.

Unlike traditional loan officers who rely strictly on tax returns and W-2 income, Joseph's approach focuses on real cash flow, income structuring, and financial strategy. He believes that borrowers should not be limited by how income is reported on paper, but instead empowered by how income is actually earned and managed.

Joseph is widely recognized for his expertise in:

• Bank statement mortgage loans• Self-employed borrower financing• Non-QM and alternative income lending• Investment property and portfolio financing• Cash-out refinance and equity strategies• Advanced mortgage loan structuring

Through his education platform, Finibi Academy, Joseph has trained tens of thousands of students worldwide in mortgage strategy, real estate investing, credit optimization, and financial independence.

He created the **Bank Statement Mortgage Loan Mastery Series** to provide a clear, step-by-step roadmap for borrowers and professionals who want to qualify for real estate without relying on traditional income documentation.

His mission is simple: To help people use their real income—not just their tax returns—to qualify, invest, and build long-term wealth.

When he is not structuring loans or writing, Joseph works with clients across the United States to design customized mortgage strategies that align with their financial goals, income structure, and long-term investment plans.

The Bank Statement Mortgage Loan Mastery Series Roadmap

The Complete Guide to Qualifying for Real Estate Using Bank Statements Instead of Tax Returns

The purpose of the **Bank Statement Mortgage Loan Mastery Series** is to give borrowers, investors, and mortgage professionals the exact strategies used by lenders and underwriters—translated into simple, practical steps you can apply in real life.

This series takes you from beginner to advanced mastery of how to qualify, structure, and scale real estate financing using bank statements instead of traditional income.

Each book builds on the last. You are not just learning how to get approved—you are learning how to control your approvals.

Book 1 — Bank Statement Mortgage Loan Fundamentals

Learn how bank statement loans work, how income is calculated, and why tax returns are no longer required for many borrowers.

Book 2 — Personal Bank Statement Mortgage Loans

Learn how to qualify using personal accounts, structure deposits, and maximize usable income.

Book 3 — Business Bank Statement Mortgage Loans

Understand how lenders analyze business revenue, apply expense ratios, and use P&Ls.

Book 4 — Bank Statement Loans for Self-Employed Borrowers

Master how entrepreneurs qualify and structure income for approval.

Book 5 — Bank Statement Loans for Primary Residences

Learn how to buy or refinance your home using bank statement income.

Book 6 — Bank Statement Loans for Investment Properties

Discover how to scale rental portfolios using bank statement + DSCR strategies.

Book 7 — Jumbo Bank Statement Mortgage Loans

Learn how to finance high-value properties with advanced requirements and structuring.

Book 8 — Bank Statement Loan Refinancing & Cash-Out Strategies

Unlock equity, reduce payments, and reinvest capital using bank statement refinancing.

Book 9 — Bank Statement Loans with Credit Challenges

Learn how to qualify even with lower credit using compensating factors and strategy.

Book 10 — Advanced Bank Statement Mortgage Loan Structuring

Engineer approvals using deposits, expense ratios, and lender guidelines.

This series is designed to move you from understanding → execution → mastery.

By the end, you will not just know how to qualify—you will know how to structure deals like a professional.

Educational & Financial Disclaimer

The **Bank Statement Mortgage Loan Mastery Series** is intended for educational and informational purposes only.

This content is designed to help readers understand bank statement mortgage lending, real estate financing strategies, and income structuring concepts. It is not financial, legal, tax, or investment advice.

Joseph G. Correa and Live Stronger Faster are not acting as your personal financial advisor, attorney, accountant, or mortgage professional through this publication.

Mortgage guidelines, underwriting standards, interest rates, and loan programs vary by lender and may change at any time without notice.

All examples in this series are for illustration purposes only and do not guarantee approval or results.

Always consult with licensed professionals before making financial decisions.

Risk Disclosure

Bank statement mortgage lending and real estate investing involve risk.

Income fluctuations, interest rate changes, market conditions, and lender guidelines can all impact loan approval and financial outcomes.

Borrowing against real estate or using leverage increases both potential returns and risks.

Failure to repay a loan may result in foreclosure and loss of property.

Cash flow, rental income, and appreciation are not guaranteed.

All strategies in this series are educational and must be evaluated based on your individual financial situation.

You are solely responsible for your financial decisions.

www.ingramcontent.com/pod-product-compliance
Lightning Source LLC
LaVergne TN
LVHW022226200926
848481LV00006B/2138
* 9 7 9 8 2 9 5 8 1 3 5 3 5 *